Alwy M. Jo

HYPOCRISY OF THE WEST SPINMEISTER

By

Alwy M. Jones

Alwy M. Jones

Buy Me Coffee

YouTube

Telegram

Alwy M. Jones

Copyright © 2024 Alwy Jones
All Rights Reserved

"If you're not careful, the newspapers will have you hating the people who are being oppressed, and loving the people who are doing the oppressing."

— **Malcolm X**

A well-functioning democracy requires politicians, media and citizens to act in good faith based on verified facts and open discourse. While political spin is inevitable, willful deception is an "existential" threat when it becomes normalized.

Newspeak and euphemisms can sugar-coat unsavory realities, such as referring to torture tactics as "enhanced interrogation" or civilian casualties as "collateral damage." Complex issues thus get reduced to simplistic sloganeering.

Deflection where valid concerns get countered with diversions or accusations of hypocrisy against critics, undermine substantive debate. Ad hominem attacks discrediting the character of opponents are also common.

The spread of misinformation and "fake news," whether intentional or not, further clouds public understanding. Social media enables wide dissemination of false or misleading narratives exploiting our cognitive biases.

The consequences of such information manipulation are severe. An ill-informed public cannot make rational decisions or hold leaders accountable. Trust in institutions erodes. Social divisions deepen as people operate based on divergent narratives.

Human rights are rights inherent to all human beings, regardless of race, sex, nationality, ethnicity, language, religion, or any other status. Human rights include the right to life and liberty, freedom from slavery and torture, freedom of opinion and expression, the right to work and education, and many more. Everyone is entitled to these rights, without discrimination.

War crime, in international law is a serious violation of the laws or customs of war as defined by international customary law and international treaties.

Genocide, the deliberate and systematic destruction of a group of people because of their ethnicity, nationality, religion, or race.

Alwy M. Jones

Massacres in Algeria - Setif and Guelma, 8th of May 1945

On May 8th 1945, in the small Algerian town of Setif, what began as celebrations marking the Allied victory over Nazi Germany took a tragic turn. As crowds of Algerian protesters marched waving Algerian flags and calling for independence from French colonial rule, clashes with the French police rapidly escalated into a bloody crackdown.

Over the next few days, violence spread to the nearby town of Guelma and surrounding areas as the French military responded with overwhelming force. Thousands of Algerian civilians were massacred, with estimates ranging up to 45,000 killed by French guns, bombs, and militia groups. Whole villages were burned to the ground in an indiscriminate campaign of violence against the local Muslim population.

For the French government, the massacres stemmed from fears of an Algerian nationalist uprising inspired by the rhetoric of liberation that followed World War II. But for Algerians, May 8th represented a breaking point where long simmering resentment against colonial oppression, economic exploitation, and institutional racism boiled over in the face of callous brutality. In the aftermath, the National Liberation Front formed as an armed rebel group aimed at driving out the French colonists and securing Algerian independence through armed revolution. This sparked an eight year war of independence that finally concluded in 1962 with Algeria achieving its sovereignty. For the local communities of Setif, Guelma and beyond, the 1945 massacres left an indelible intergenerational trauma. Families lost husbands, fathers, sons and brothers to the French violence. Oral histories passed down still speak of the horror of that day and the scars never healed.

While the massacres solidified Algerian resolve for self-determination, their cruelty also revealed the moral bankruptcy of the French colonial project in Algeria. After over a century of repressive imperial rule that profited from Algerian land and labor, the events of May 1945 starkly exposed the lengths to which the colonial regime would go to maintain its power and control. In this light, the Setif and Guelma massacres stand as a tragic yet pivotal inflection point in Algeria's struggle for independence from France. The appalling violence tore away any remaining fiction of a benevolent or civilizing aspect to colonial dominion. In its wake, the yearning for freedom and national dignity ignited into a conflagration that could not be extinguished until liberation was achieved in 1962.

Today, as Algeria commemorates its hard-won independence every May 8th, the memorials and vigils serve as solemn reminders of the immense sacrifice and suffering Algerians endured on the path to self-determination. And more broadly, the massacres of 1945 exemplify the brutal, dehumanizing reality of colonial subjugation, a history that continues to resonate as the legacies of empire are reckoned with globally.

French soldiers stand in front of the many Algerians they massacred in 1945

French soldiers standing in front of Algerians, massacred in 1945

Algerians, Massacred in 1945 by French Soldiers.

Alwy M. Jones

The Massacre that Ignited Angola's War

On a sunny morning in the village of Nambuangongo, northern Angola, hundreds of peaceful protesters gathered, waving banners calling for Angolan independence from Portugal's brutal colonial rule. They sang songs and chanted nationalist slogans inspired by the wave of liberation movements sweeping across Africa in the early 1960s. But their dream of freedom was about to turn into a nightmare.

As the crowds continued swelling, Portuguese police reinforcements were called in, joined by feared colonial militia groups. Without warning, the security forces opened fire indiscriminately on the demonstrators massacring men, women and children with horrific disregard for human life. Contemporary accounts describe a sustained hail of gunfire and frantic crowds fleeing only to be cut down mercilessly.

When the shooting finally ceased hours later, the scale of the atrocity became clear. Official reports listed over 300 Angolans dead, but firsthand accounts suggest the true death toll stretched into the thousands, with as many as 5,000 massacred that day.

The savagery of the Nambuangongo massacre represented a point of no return for Angola's independence struggle against Portugal's repressive colonial regime. What was once a largely peaceful movement turned increasingly militant in the wake of such abhorrent state violence against civilians. The massacre helped catalyze the formation and growth of rebel groups like the Popular Movement for the Liberation of Angola and National Union for the Total Independence of Angola who took up arms to force the Portuguese out by any means necessary.

For the rural communities around Nambuangongo, the massacre left deep painful scars. Whole families and villages lost their lives in the space of a morning. The trauma resonated for generations amid the ensuing decades of armed conflict, instability and violence as Angola's grueling war for independence raged on.

In many ways, the Nambuangongo massacre served as a catalyst for this bitter struggle that finally led to Angolan independence in 1975 after centuries under Portugal's colonial yoke. Its horror exposed beyond doubt the lengths the Portuguese authoritarian regime would go to brutally suppress the nationalist aspirations of Angolans and other colonial subjects across its African continent.

As Angola still grapples with the legacy of that violent conflict today, the tragedy of Nambuangongo remains seared into the national psyche. An enduring memorial complex now stands on the massacre site, with mass graves holding remains of the fallen. Each year on March 15th, the day is commemorated across Angola and the diaspora as both a reminder of the heavy sacrifices paid on the road to liberation and a rallying cry to uphold and defend the hard won freedoms of an independent Angola.

Alwy M. Jones

The Punitive Pillage of Benin City: Britain's Bloody Conquest of 1897

In February 1897, a well-armed British expeditionary force prepared to invade the Kingdom of Benin, a powerful West African state whose highly-developed artistic, political and economic systems dated back to the 13th century. The official pretext was to avenge the killing of a British expedition party that had violated Benin's sovereignty a few months earlier. But the real motivation underlying this "Punitive Expedition" was Britain's relentless colonial thirst for territorial expansion, natural resources, and subjugation of independent African kingdoms.

After weeks of military preparations, the British force of 1,200 soldiers, marines launched their assault on Benin City. They encountered fierce resistance from the highly-skilled Benin warriors who defended their capital with a bravery and determination that briefly stunned the British forces. However, the Benin forces were no match for the British firepower of artillery, maxim guns, and modern explosives.

In the battle's aftermath, a victorious yet undisciplined British force exacted its terrible revenge. For days, Benin City was systematically pillaged, looted, and burned by rampaging British troops. They desecrated ceremonial monuments, set homes and sacred sites ablaze, and committed unspeakable atrocities against civilians. An irreplaceable trove of Benin's renowned bronzes, ivories, and artworks was plundered to be cruelly displayed as trophies of conquest in Britain for decades to come.

As word spread of the sacking of their capital, an untold number of surrounding towns and villages were abandoned by Benin's traumatized people as they fled into the forests and swamps to escape the dread of the British invaders. Those who remained were brutalized, arrested, and conscripted into forced labor to serve British colonial interests.

In one massacre alone, British troops were credibly accused of killing at least 500 civilians who had taken refuge in Benin City's main bazaar and mosque courtyard. Elderly men, women, and children were cut down in the indiscriminate violence.

For the colonial officers who orchestrated the Expedition, the officially stated aim of "removing obstacles" to expanding British control over the lucrative natural resources of the Niger Coast Protectorate was achieved through overwhelming military force. In reality, this showcased the brutality of late 19th century European colonialism driven by the toxic combination of greed, racism, and arrogant notions of cultural superiority.

In the decades that followed the Expedition, the mighty Kingdom of Benin never recovered. Its monarchy, culture, and sovereignty were dismantled and absorbed into the British colonial system until Nigeria achieved independence in 1960. Countless irreplaceable artworks and priceless artifacts stolen from Benin remain held in Western museums to this day, despite calls for their repatriation.

For the Edo people of Benin, the traumatic invasion of 1897 left a deep imprint that still lingers. The event is remembered in oral histories as the "day everything ended" when their once prosperous and advanced society was destroyed by the depravities of British colonial conquest.

More broadly, the Benin Expedition served as an ignominious example of Europe's exerting its military dominance to feed an endless appetite for acquiring overseas territories, resources, and forced subjugation of indigenous peoples. It showed in brutal fashion how the racist doctrine of White supremacy fueled moral atrocities and cultural desecration on an industrial scale in the colonial era.

Today, as the world grapples with legacies of colonialism, imperialism, and systemic racism, the destruction visited upon the Kingdom of Benin stands as a haunting parable for the violent excesses and injustices perpetrated in the pursuit of the colonial project. The resilience of Benin's cultural identity and calls for reparations also reflect the enduring struggles over truth, justice, and reconciliation that still reverberate in our modern world.

King Leopold's Terrifying Reign of Rubber Terror

From 1885 to 1908, the Congo Free State belonged to King Leopold II of Belgium as his personal fiefdom and private rubber plantation. What followed was a reign of human exploitation, savagery and greed unparalleled on the African continent. Millions of Congolese men, women and children suffered unbearable cruelties or died at the hands of the ruthless colonial regime.

The driving force behind this institutionalized campaign of terror was rubber; the vital raw material that enriched Leopold and his financial cartel of investors. Congolese villages were forced into providing quotas of this lucrative natural rubber to the Belgian authorities through a system of hostage-taking, mutilations and murder on a horrendous scale.

Those who failed to meet the crushing rubber quotas faced punitive reprisals. Homes were looted and torched. Entire villages were massacred and displaced. This extreme violence was meted out by the brutal Belgian militia and their mercenary armies.

One of the most chilling techniques used was the severing of hands or limbs as a means of enforcing the rubber regimen. Surviving accounts describe how severed hands were dried, smoked and even traded as a grim currency to show village rubber quotas were met through such butchery.

Overall death tolls from disease, overwork, famine, and violence are still debated, but the lowest estimates surpass 5 million Congolese killed; over half the country's population at the time. Some scholars allege a staggering 10-15 million died during Leopold's reign, putting the Congo atrocities on par with other modern genocides in terms of lives lost through calculated brutality and neglect.

Despite attempts to censor details, outsiders managed to expose the staggering human toll and mobilize an international movement against Leopold's excesses.

In the aftermath, the scars of Leopold's rubber terror lingered for generations across Congolese society. Whole ethnic groups like the Ndundu were exterminated. Cultural knowledge, social stability and prosperity reversed decades of advancement. The cycle of conflict, displacement and instability continues to this day, compounded by external corporate exploitation of the Congo's vast natural resources.

Many historians and scholars argue that the Congo atrocities represented the most brutal excesses of European colonialism and unregulated corporate greed on the African continent. Not only was its scale of death and destruction unmatched, but the purposeful savagery defied the supposed "civilizing mission" used to justify the colonization of Africa in the first place.

In modern times, calls for reparations, repatriating looted art, and official apologies from Belgium have only grown louder. The generational harms inflicted during Leopold's Congo nightmare continue radiating through Congolese society and economy due to the country's destabilization and the disrupted development of civil society.

The Congo atrocities stand as a supremely shameful chapter in the annals of colonialism and corporate overreach when one European monarch and his capitalist court enriched themselves through systematized terror, theft of resources, and the dehumanization of millions of Africans. And yet, these preventable massacres and crimes against humanity were obscured for far too long by official silence and censorship; an injustice now being reckoned with globally.

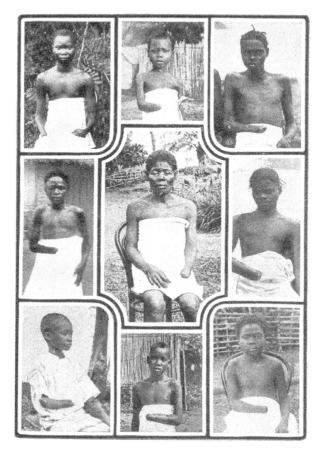

Mutilated Congolese children and adults (c. 1900-1905) — in Congo Free State (present-day Democratic Republic of the Congo) Privately owned territory of Belgian King Leopold II, with numerous enslaved rubber collection/production areas in the rainforest and on plantations.

A missionary holds up a Congolese man's arm at the elbow, and points to villager's missing hand.

Ethiopia's Day of Martyrdom and Defiance

On February 19th 1937, the streets of Addis Ababa ran red with the blood of Ethiopian civilians gunned down by Italian occupying forces. This date, known as Yekatit 12 on the Ethiopian calendar, would become enshrined as a day of martyrdom and resistance during the tragic period of Fascist Italy's occupation.

The events of Yekatit 12 were precipitated by growing tensions and resentment in the capital against the cruel policies of Italian viceroy Rodolfo Graziani and his desires to brutally subjugate the Ethiopian population. Minor clashes and acts of defiance by Ethiopians against the oppressive Italian rulers increased in the days prior.

On the morning of February 19th, attempts by Italian soldiers to arrest Ethiopian monks and students escalated into a full-blown confrontation at the capital's Yekatit 12 square and surrounding environs. Gunfire broke out, and the Italians soon indiscriminately turned their weapons on the civilian population.

For three horrifying days, innocent men, women, and children were massacred by Italian soldiers and artillery raining down on the city. Historians estimate at least 19,000 unarmed Ethiopian civilians were killed, while some accounts claim over 30,000 lost their lives with many more injured during the retaliatory slaughter.

Among those martyred were esteemed members of Ethiopia's intellectual class; scholars, writers, poets, aristocrats who were rounded up and summarily executed by the Italian fascists intent on decapitating Ethiopia's national identity and spirit of independence.

Emperor Haile Selassie, who had previously fled the country to plead for international assistance, memorably called Yekatit 12 "one of the most horrifying massacres of modern times." Indeed, the atrocity was a shocking escalation even by the standards of the violent Italian campaign to colonize Ethiopia, which had already caused tremendous death and displacement.

Yet from the ashes of Yekatit 12, the spirit of resistance and Ethiopian defiance only strengthened, spurring on liberation movements that continued battling Italian occupation for years to come. The date became emblazoned as a galvanizing symbol of national martyrdom, a rallying cry for the struggle to reclaim Ethiopia's sovereignty and freedom.

Even after Italian forces were finally driven out in 1941 after five years of occupation, Yekatit 12 remained enshrined as Ethiopia's day to memorialize and honor the sacrifices made for independence. Annual commemorations feature solemn memorial services, ceremonial re-enactments of defiant acts, and continued calls for "never again" to allow such a national tragedy.

At its core, Yekatit 12 epitomized the violent excesses and racist brutality of European fascism's drive to conquer and subjugate sovereign African nations like Ethiopia. The date represents one of the single greatest losses of civilian life at the hands of occupying forces in Ethiopia. But it just as powerfully embodied the indomitable Ethiopian national spirit of resistance that ultimately prevailed against oppression and genocide.

Today, the memorials and monuments of Yekatit 12 stand as haunting reminders of the heavy sacrifice of lives lost, while inspiring continued vigilance against injustice and the struggle to protect Ethiopia's hard-won independence and autonomy from any force that would compromise it, whether domestic or foreign.

February 19, 1937: Yekatit 12 Massacre of more than 19,000 Ethiopians.

Pidjiguiti: The Catalyst for Guinea Bissau's Liberation Struggle

On August 3, 1959, the village of Pidjiguiti in what was then Portuguese Guinea became the bloody crucible where the embers of Guinea Bissau's independence movement were stoked into an inferno. A peaceful protest by dock workers demanding better labor conditions from their Portuguese colonial overseers was met with horrific violence that catalyzed wider nationalist sentiments.

That fateful morning, hundreds of dockworkers from the Pidjiguiti harbor had congregated to March and rally for improved pay and working hours. However, when Portuguese military police attempted to violently disperse the crowds, chaotic clashes erupted. Gunfire broke out, with the heavily outmatched protesters.

Reinforcements were swiftly called in, and what followed was a brutal crackdown as Portuguese forces indiscriminately opened fire on Pidjiguiti with machine guns, grenades, and even naval artillery from warships anchored offshore. Civilians fleeing were shot, homes were burnt, and an untold number massacred over the ensuing days.

While official Portuguese figures admitted to around 50 casualties, firsthand accounts from survivors suggest the true death toll reached into the thousands dead in the coastal town by the time the smoke cleared. Dozens more went missing, likely among the corpses burnt or dumped into the harbor.

The sheer savagery of the Portuguese response transformed a relatively minor labor dispute into a catalyzing historical event that sparked widespread outrage across Portuguese Guinea. For the burgeoning independence movement led by future president Amilcar Cabral and his African Party for the Independence of Guinea and Cape Verde, Pidjiguiti became akin to Sharpeville in South Africa; a turning point where demands for gradual reforms gave way to a steadfast conviction that only armed revolution could overthrow Portuguese colonial oppression.

"Pidjiguiti exposed the Portuguese regime's brutality and opened the eyes of our people to just how little value was placed on African life," Cabral declared at the time. "It became obvious the path to liberation from this racist tyranny would not be peaceful."

In the aftermath, PAIGC militants gained newfound support across Guinea as news of the Pidjiguiti massacre spread. Peasant and worker groups flocked to join the burgeoning rebel effort which finally erupted into full-scale guerrilla war against Portuguese rule in 1963.

For over a decade, PAIGC forces waged a grueling armed campaign that gradually decolonized swaths of the country from Lisbon's control at immense human cost. Villages were razed, civilians massacred, and scorched earth tactics used by both sides during the bitter independence struggle.

Finally in 1974, the Carnation Revolution in Portugal removed its authoritarian Estado Novo government from power. With Portugal now willing to decolonize, Guinea-Bissau achieved its long-sought independence later that year stemming from the Pindjiguiti catalyst.

Even today, Guinea-Bissau's modern history remains profoundly shaped by the events of that August morning in 1959. The date is commemorated each year to honor the martyrs who were slain in one of the worst Portuguese colonial massacres, while celebrating their sacrifices that drove the country's successful liberation decades later.

Pidjiguiti also underscored the depth of Portugal's unwillingness to pursue any path of peaceful decolonization; a reality that became evident across its other African territories where likewise brutal suppression of independence movements provoked protracted anti-colonial conflicts from Angola to Mozambique.

For this former Portuguese colony, the trauma of Pidjiguiti lent credence to Cabral's conviction that armed struggle was the only way forward. And though the birth of an independent Guinea-Bissau was inevitably achieved, the scars of this violent inception still reverberate through a nation still grappling with the aftermath of its hard-fought liberation over half a century later.

The Sotik Massacre: Kenya's Brutal Awakening to Colonial Oppression

On the morning of March 19th 1905, a British patrol consisting of 34 soldiers entered the village of Sotik in the fertile highlands west of modern day Nairobi. Their mission was to apprehend a local Kisii chief, Olemasogo, who had defied orders to join a forced labor brigade constructing a road for colonial infrastructure projects.

What unfolded over the ensuring hours represented one of the first major massacres perpetrated by British imperialists against indigenous Kenyans; a shocking catalyst that exposed the brutal lengths the colonial regime would take to subjugate the local population through violence and intimidation.

As the soldiers approached Chief Olemasogo's homestead, gunfire erupted from the village's warriors attempting to resist the arrest and protect their leader. Though outmatched, the Kisii tribesmen fought fiercely, stoking the wrath of the British commander who rallied his troops and began indiscriminately firing into the village with rifles and machine guns.

By the end of the one sided clash, as many as 1,500 Kisii villagers lay dead according to oral histories, including many women, children and the elderly. The surviving warriors finally fled into surrounding forests, forced to abandon their burning homes and loved ones' corpses. Only a handful of British were injured.

In the wake of the massacre, British authorities made little attempt to conceal or deny what had occurred. The colonial government instead cast the Sotik killings as a necessary and justified response to put down "savagery" and ensure imperial writ extended across the colony's highlands.

For the indigenous inhabitants of the fertile Rift Valley region like the Kisii, Maasai and Nandi peoples, the sheer scale of violence visited upon Sotik by their British colonizers marked a turning point. Gone were any illusions of benevolent British rule or a "civilizing mission." Instead, the oppression, displacement and depredations of harsh colonial economic policies was now backed by the capability and willingness to unleash indiscriminate destruction on any who resisted.

In many ways, Sotik proved to be a harbinger of decades of subsequent colonial conflict, land alienation and subjugation still to come in British Kenya. The tactics of collective punishment, scorch earth policies and disproportionate military responses to even minor resistance would become horrifically familiar.

This bitterly seared into the Kenyan psyche an understanding that the colonial enterprise was not a noble civilizing force, but an entirely extractive regime where indigenous lives and rights meant nothing compared to British economic interests and total domination.

Ultimately the Sotik Massacre represented a seminal catalyst in the long Kenyan freedom struggle against British imperialism; one which would simmer for decades through cycles of upheaval, armed insurrections and oppression before finally achieving independence in 1963. Yet even today, Sotik remains enshrined in collective memory as a powerful symbol of the inhumanity, racism and violence that defined colonial rule across Kenya and much of Africa.

Seen through this lens, the tragedy of March 19, 1905 stands as an early example of how the European colonial project's rhetoric of "civilizing" was a duplicitous façade; one that routinely gave way to the unbridled savagery of massacres like Sotik when indigenous Africans dared defy economic subjugation. Such wanton violence betrayed the true coercive nature of imperialism in Kenya and set an ominous precedent for the trials still to come in dismantling the British Empire on African soil.

Alwy M. Jones

The Mau Mau War and Its Lingering Scars

From 1952 to 1960, the forests and villages of central Kenya were torn apart by a brutal conflict pitting British colonial forces against the defiant Mau Mau rebel movement demanding independence and a return of seized land. What became known as the Mau Mau Uprising or Kenya Emergency left a lasting impact through its cycles of insurgency, scorched earth reprisals, civilian massacres and systematic human rights abuses.

At its core, the Mau Mau rebellion erupted from long-simmering Kikuyu grievances over village land being seized for British settlers, as well as resentment towards economic and political disenfranchisement under colonial rule. As resistance stiffened, British authorities declared a State of Emergency and initiated a campaign of violence intended to crush Mau Mau fighters and suppress broader nationalist aims.

Over the following years, many atrocities were committed which scarred the Kenyan people. The rebel Mau Mau were infamous for orchestrating gruesome oath taking and killings of fellow Kikuyu deemed loyalists. An undetermined number of settlers and tribal "home guards" also fell victim to their guerilla attacks.

In response, British forces demonstrated an utter disregard for civilian lives as entire villages were razed and their occupants interned in appalling conditions at prison camps like Hola and Bura. Torture and killings were widespread, with thousands of deaths occurring in these detention centers through illness, mistreatment and violence by British guards. Many elderly Kenyans can still recount horrifying stories from the atrocities they witnessed.

One of the darkest chapters involved the notorious "screening" camps where suspects endured whippings, beatings, sexual assault and other tortures to extract confessions of Mau Mau ties. These interrogation tactics, partly conducted by colonial counter-insurgency methods first deployed during Britain's wartime occupation of Nazi Germany, represented one of the most egregious instances of institutional human rights abuses in the dying years of the British Empire.

Even outside the camps, whole tracts of countryside were depopulated through forced relocation schemes. Meanwhile, indiscriminate killings, reprisal massacres like those in Kiambu in 1953, and wanton destruction by British forces alienated much of the Kikuyu population and increasingly turned rural sympathies towards the Mau Mau.

By the time the rebellion was finally crushed in 1960 and Kenya achieved independence three years later, the human toll on the colony had been catastrophic. Estimates of Kenyan deaths range from tens to over one hundred thousand from violence, displacement or detentions. With several horrific incidents like the

Hola Massacre memorialized as exemplifying the British campaign's depravity.

Beyond the bodily costs, the psychological and cultural impacts were also severe. Whole tracts of central Kenya remain pockmarked by abandoned villages, mass graves and detention camp sites. Survivors recount heartbreaking stories of wives, children and parents killed or disappeared. The trauma radiated through generations in the form of poverty, land disputes, broken ancestral lines and loss of cultural identity.

In the decades since independence, the Mau Mau struggle and its martyrs have gradually become recognized as a powerful symbol of Kenyan nationalism, resilience and sacrifice as they fought to reclaim stolen land and secure self-rule. However, attempts to properly memorialize or reckon with this difficult period were long obstructed by British intransigence and institutional silence.

It was not until the 21st century that Britain finally began formally acknowledging culpability for abuses and massacres committed by its colonial forces during the uprising. Protracted legal campaigns by Kenyan survivors ultimately forced an official apology and compensation package from the British government. Historians were also finally granted access to long concealed archival evidence detailing the full scope of atrocities.

Even still, many see these concessions as far too little, too late. The British narratives around the conflict and myth of the Mau Mau as a murderous cult caused willful amnesia around its legitimate anti-colonial grievances and Britain's own institutional racism. In Kenya itself, some still view the Mau Mau's violent rebellion as a source of national shame rather than a catalyst for liberation from injustice.

Regardless, the indelible imprint of the Mau Mau war remains etched upon Kenya's soul and the generational trauma continues radiating outwards in the form of land disputes, poverty, unhealed wounds and simmering grievances. As the country strives to reckon with this turbulent past, the massacres and indignities inflicted during these darkest days of British imperial rule cast an inescapable pall over modern Kenya representing an origin story born in blood, struggle and sacrifice that cannot be forgotten.

Alwy M. Jones

The Chuka Massacre: A Bloody Stain on Kenya's Colonial Legacy

On the morning of June 25th 1953, the village of Chuka in Kenya's fertile Highlands erupted in chaos and bloodshed. Over the course of a few horrific hours, at least 100 Kenyan civilians primarily Igembe men, women and children from the local Meru community were massacred by British colonial troops.

The violence represented one of the single worst atrocities committed by British forces during the Mau Mau Uprising that raged across Kenya from 1952-1960. Yet even decades later, the full scale of the Chuka Massacre and efforts to uncover the truth remain obscured and unresolved.

The roots of the tragedy lie in the escalating Mau Mau rebellion, as Kikuyu militants sought to reclaim appropriated ancestral lands and overthrow British colonial rule through armed struggle. Though not directly involved, communities like the Igembe in Chuka found themselves caught in the middle, viewed with suspicion by British authorities.

On that fateful June morning, a small patrol of British troops entered Chuka following an alleged incident where a military convoy had come under fire nearby. Almost immediately, the situation destabilized into a frenzy of violence with soldiers from the King's African Rifles indiscriminately opening fire on Igembe villagers, in homes, farms and even at a local nursery school.

Survivors recount a horrifying scene of mayhem as bullets rained from all directions. Some were gunned down fleeing, while many were killed attempting to take cover inside mud huts that were then set ablaze by the attackers. Children were not spared, resulting in entire families being wiped out.

Even after the massacres ceased, the British colonial administration made efforts to systematically cover up the scale of the atrocities. Official accounts drastically underplayed the death toll at merely 20 killed. Many bodies were hastily burned to eliminate evidence.

It was not until survivor testimonies surfaced decades later that the true horrors of Chuka came into focus, detailing how up to 150 men, women and children of the Igembe people may have died in just those few fateful hours. Other records revealed the British had immediately imposed a strict media blackout and curfew to contain any reporting of the event.

In the aftermath, the once prosperous Igembe community in Chuka never fully recovered. Displaced villagers feared returning due to the brutality, resulting in a diaspora across Kenya and beyond. Witnesses' recounted nightmares, trauma, and lost livelihoods stemming from the massacres. Many bodies were never recovered or buried, leaving relatives without closure.

Subsequent British investigations concluded that the troops likely resorted to indiscriminate and disproportionate killings in retaliation for the attack on the military convoy. However, no colonial soldiers faced prosecution over the civilian massacre, with the British postwar administration in Kenya making little effort to reckon with such excesses.

It was not until Kenya's independence in 1963 that they apologized for the massacre and recognized the Chuka dead with a memorial monument in the village. But broader investigations and truth telling efforts have remained stymied over the decades by lost records, stonewalling from British authorities, and the difficulties of gathering evidence over sixty years on.

Even today, the Chuka Massacre remains an open wound for many Kenyans, representing the brutal savagery inflicted upon civilians amid the struggles to overturn colonial subjugation. As the country continues reckoning with this difficult chapter, calls have grown for the British government to finally reckon with its obfuscation of the truth and potentially pursue of belated legal proceedings.

At its core, Chuka exemplified how British "civilizing" forces demonstrated a stunning degree of casual disregard for the very African lives they claimed to be uplifting. In response to militant uprising, a monstrous colonial overreaction enabled the very dehumanization and mass violence it rhetorically sought to transcend.

Alwy M. Jones

Reckoning with the Hola Massacre

On March 3rd 1959, in the remote Hola Desert of Kenya's North Eastern Province, British colonial forces perpetrated one of the most notorious atrocities during the bloody Mau Mau rebellion. At the Hola Detention Camp, Colonial authorities brutally assaulted and killed dozens of civilian internees in an incident that sparked international outrage and further exposed the savagery underpinning Britain's iron-fisted efforts to crush the anti-colonial uprising.

The catalyst for the violence came when a group of 85 detainees initially refused to work in the camp's quarries that day as a protest over their continued internment. In response, British prison wardens and members of the notorious Kikuyu Home Guard auxiliary force descended on the prisoners with truncheons, clubs and other weapons.

What ensued was a gruesome hours-long frenzy of beatings and whippings inflicted on the defenseless detainees. Contemporary accounts describe men and boys being struck indiscriminately on their heads, groins, and stomachs. Some were singled out for especially harsh floggings until they lost consciousness or were killed outright.

By the time the beatings finally ceased, 11 men had been beaten to death with dozens more left severely injured, some with permanent disabilities. The graphic images of distended bodies and the extent of the cruelty later sparked revulsion among European colonial officials and the global public when they came to light.

For authorities overseeing the network of harsh detention camps, the Hola Massacre represented a brutal exemplar of the dehumanizing conditions Kenyan internees endured; both at the hands of sadistic British wardens and from the Kikuyu tribal "home guard" forces recruited to terrorize their own countrymen. Torture, disease, overcrowding, and summary killings were rampant throughout the camps established to hold suspected Mau Mau rebels and sympathizers.

In the direct aftermath of Hola, the senior warden in charge of the camp and governor of the detention program were dismissed in an attempt at damage control. However, no British prison staff ever faced any legal consequences for the killings, with official reports whitewashing the death toll down to "just" 11 killed.

In Kenya itself, the massacre further confirmed for many that the only path to self-determination required decisive military victory over the British colonial forces capable of such wanton violence. For the rebel Mau Mau fighters continuing their guerrilla war, Hola served as a searing rallying cry to press the struggle aware of the inhumane treatment they could expect if captured by British forces.

Even after Kenya achieved independence in 1963, the legacies of Hola persisted in corroding the credibility of British colonial narratives around ostensibly "humane" policies for subduing the Mau Mau insurgency. As more details emerged, including damning evidence and testimonies that the British had actively suppressed, the atrocities proved too grave to dismiss.

In more recent years, legal and political campaigns by surviving Hola victims and Mau Mau veterans finally pressured the British government into an official apology in 2013 and a compensation fund for remaining survivors of the colonial detention program.

However, many Kenyans feel justice and accountability remain incomplete nearly 65 years after Hola. There are still demands for further investigations into undocumented deaths at other camps, the release of all remaining classified British archives on the Mau Mau crisis, and even potential criminal prosecutions if evidence of systematic human rights abuses by colonial authorities is uncovered.

Additionally, efforts continue to memorialize the victims of the massacre itself. In 2015, Hola's mass gravesite was accorded national monument status by Kenyan authorities, with annual commemorations held each year. A museum exploring the grim history of the detention camps is also being planned.

Though over half a century has passed, the trauma of Hola remains an open wound for many Kenyans a searing reminder of the inhumanity and racism that enabled such abhorrent colonial violence. As a new generation grapples with its national liberation's bloody origins, the massacre stands as a singularly dark exemplar of the horrors perpetrated in British Kenya to crush aspirations of self-determination. Only by truly reckoning with and memorializing atrocities like Hola can this indelible stain on the colonial era's human rights record begin fading from the ongoing struggles over historical truth, justice and a common humanity.

Alwy M. Jones

Shar al-Shatt: Libya's Bloody Baptism of Italian Conquest

On October 23rd 1911, the Ottoman ruled province of Tripolitania in what is now western Libya became the scene of one of the first major massacres and atrocities of Europe's unseemly scramble to carve up the African continent through brute military force.

Only a month after the Italian kingdom had launched an invasion to wrest control of the provinces of Tripolitania and Cyrenaica from the Ottoman Empire, a large force of over 10,000 Italian soldiers and sailors approached the desert town of Shar al-Shatt, just inland from the Mediterranean coast. Their mission was to secure the area as a future base of operations in their newly launched war of colonial conquest.

Unknown to the Italians, the local population had rallied a substantial force to defend their homes and families from the foreign invaders. In concealed positions at an oasis outside Shar al-Shatt, over 1,500 defiant Libyans consisting of Ottoman troops, Bedouin fighters and villagers waited to ambush the encroaching Italians.

In the ensuing battle on October 23rd, Italian forces were initially caught off-guard by the heavy resistance as the Libyan defensive positions opened up with rifle and artillery fire, inflicting casualties. However, the ambush was finally broken after a lengthy exchange when Italian naval gunboats offshore began indiscriminately bombarding the Libyan positions and nearby village with heavy shelling.

As smoke cleared, the Italian troops pushed into the shattered village of Shar al-Shatt, where horrific scenes of carnage awaited them. Rather than take prisoners, the enraged Italian soldiers set upon the remaining Libyan survivors killing men, women and children indiscriminately out of a perceived sense of retribution.

While precise figures are still debated, it's estimated that between 500-700 Libyan civilians and fighters were massacred in cold blood at Shar al-Shatt by the vengeful Italian forces. Few prisoners were taken, with even the wounded left behind as the victors pillaged the destroyed village.

Though a relatively obscure battle by modern standards, Shar al-Shatt proved to be a watershed moment for Libya's anti-colonial struggle against Italy's belated imperial ambitions. The sheer brutality of the massacre exposed for Libyans the remorseless violence the Italian invaders were willing to inflict upon civilians to achieve conquest. It galvanized wider resistance to the invasion throughout Tripolitania and Cyrenaica.

In the months and years that followed, the Italians would continue resorting to tactics of reprisal killings, scorched earth policies, and concentration camps to eventually crush the Libyan uprising by 1923. But the Shar al-Shatt massacre represented an opening salvo that radicalized the Libyan resistance from mere

Ottoman defense into a people's struggle for national liberation from Italy's expansionist designs.

The date would eventually become enshrined into the modern Libyan consciousness as a seminal blood sacrifice that laid the foundations for its ultimate independence achieved after decades of struggle and strife against the often brutal realities of Italian colonization.

More broadly, Shar al-Shatt also exemplified how the European powers deploying "civilizing missions" as a pretext for seizing African lands in the early 20th century was often exposed as rank hypocrisy at best and unapologetic savagery at worst. From Shar al-Shatt to Omdurman and beyond, colonial militaries demonstrated they were quite willing to perpetrate massacres against occupied peoples in order to subjugate them under imperial control.

In this light, the events of that harrowing October day in 1911 in a remote Libyan desert have become emblematic of the violent birth pangs of national liberation movements rising across Africa fueled by resistance to such calculated atrocities. Though largely overlooked in the face of larger battles in the World Wars that followed, Shar al-Shatt remains profoundly symbolic as perhaps the first major colonial massacre to plant the seeds of a proud nation's long struggle against European subjugation that eventually blossomed in Libya's hard fought independence.

Alwy M. Jones

Madagascar's Wounds of Colonialism: Reckoning with the Legacy of the 1947 Massacres

On March 29th 1947, the Indian Ocean island of Madagascar became the site of one of the 20th century's most brutal and under-reported colonial massacres. On that fateful spring day, French military forces launched a coordinated assault on towns and villages across the Malagasy hinterlands where an independence movement and uprising was unfolding.

What ensued was a horrific frenzy of violence as French troops and armed colonial settlers indiscriminately gunned down men, women and children in residential areas and public spaces. Homes were set ablaze, summary executions were widespread, and towns were bombed and razed to the ground in a campaign of retribution and collective punishment nominally aimed at crushing the Malagasy uprising.

By the time the massacres finally ceased weeks later, credible estimates indicate at least 100,000 Malagasy civilians had perished at the hands of French forces. Countless more were wounded, displaced or left destitute as entire communities were wiped from the map.

For the Malagasy people, this represented an apocalyptic ethnic and cultural trauma on a scale unmatched by few other colonial atrocities in Africa in terms of lives lost. Whole families and ancestral lineages were exterminated in entire regions of the island.

Yet in the wake of the massacres, French colonial authorities made concerted efforts to censor, obfuscate and downplay the true scale of their retaliatory violence. Official records listed the civilian death toll at only around 8,000; a deliberately deceptive accounting that failed to capture the true horrors visited upon the Malagasy people. An entire nation's story of suffering was whitewashed from history.

It was only in the 21st century that the full magnitude of the 1947 massacres finally resurfaced in the Malagasy national consciousness. As archives were gradually declassified and survivor accounts meticulously compiled over decades, a more complete portrait of devastation emerged triggering impassioned calls for truth and reparations.

In particular, detailed accounts of French culpability from military officers and civilian witnesses confirming large-scale civilian killings and destruction of villages sent shockwaves across Madagascar and the international community. The censored histories gave way to a fuller reckoning with the inhumanity and racial animus underpinning the colonial regime's brutality.

Today, the date of March 29th remains a complex and fraught subject on the island. For the Merina ethnic highlanders who bore the worst of the massacres, the date serves as a national day of mourning and remembrance. Commemorations have become widespread featuring vigils, speeches, and ceremonies at mass grave sites memorializing the nameless and countless victims.

At the same time, voices across Madagascar and among the global diaspora have elevated demands for France to properly acknowledge its role, apologize, and potentially provide some form of restitution for the descendants of the massacres' victims. The French government has so far resisted such measures or formal investigations into the 1947 events.

For its part, the Malagasy state has pursued a form of transitional justice through official truth and reconciliation commissions, public teaching curriculums, and symbolic reparations measures aimed at healing the traumatic legacy of the colonial-era massacres.

However, generational fissures and simmering resentments toward France still remain amid ongoing debates over the massacres' rightful place in Madagascar's national consciousness. Some view lingering French cultural and economic influence as an impediment to fully moving forward.

Regardless of the complexities, the resurfaced histories of the 1947 massacres in Madagascar have become deeply embedded as a powerful synecdoche for the towering human costs of colonialism, ethno-racial subjugation, and the continent's struggle for liberation from imperial domination.

The sheer scale of death represents a searing reminder of the horrific extremes and violence to which colonizing powers were willing to resort in order to preserve their dominion even against civilian populations simply demanding sovereignty over their lands and lives.

Through this lens, the March 29th massacres have become a cornerstone tragedy in Madagascar's national story; one representing the immense suffering and sacrifice endured for achieving independence later in 1960. But they also epitomize a larger human struggle for truth, accountability and restorative justice in the face of historical atrocities too long suppressed in the shadows of empire.

Malawi's Anti-Colonial Uprising

On the night of January 15th 1915, John Chilembwe, a Baptist minister and educator, raised the banner of armed insurrection against British colonial rule over the territory of Nyasaland. Alongside a small band of followers, he launched a bold but doomed attack on a plantation and colonial outposts around his village of Mbombwe, an act representing one of the earliest anti-colonial uprisings across Africa.

While ultimately crushed within weeks by British troops, Chilembwe's revolt from that January evening would reverberate across decades as a potent symbol of Malawian resistance to oppressive foreign domination. It was both the harbinger of wider nationalist awakenings to come, as well as a searing indictment of the violence and exploitation underpinning colonial subjugation.

For Chilembwe, a path toward open confrontation with British authorities had been steadily charted over years of witnessing the quotidian indignities, deprivations and cruelties inflicted upon his fellow Africans by the colonial system. Despite establishing a mission and school teaching self-determination, he increasingly became radicalized by draconian labor policies and land seizures by British plantation corporations. The harsh mistreatment of a well-educated Chilembwe by racist colonial administrators further stoked his revolutionary fervor.

When World War I erupted in 1914 and many British colonists left Nyasaland to join the war effort, Chilembwe identified an opportune moment for open revolt. After months of secret plotting and militant recruitment, his group launched coordinated attacks on a munitions depot and two plantations around Mbombwe on January 15th 1915. Three white settlers were killed and temporary control of the area was seized.

In response, British troops and police swiftly mobilized reinforcements and artillery to crush the uprising through overwhelming firepower. Days of conflict ensued with the rebel force badly outmatched. On January 26th, Chilembwe's remaining followers and family were cornered at his church where many, including his wife and daughter, died in a final clash.

Chilembwe himself managed to flee into the wilderness but was eventually tracked down, captured and unceremoniously executed by firing squad on February 3rd 1915. His body was buried in an unmarked grave; a symbolic suppression of his subversive uprising against colonial authority.

In the aftermath, a harsh wave of retaliatory executions, detentions and collective punishments were inflicted across Nyasaland. Over 300 Africans were condemned to death by colonial tribunals with entire villages razed. The British swiftly moved to erase any public memory of Chilembwe's defiance.

However, the martyr seeds of resistance had been firmly planted. Over the coming decades, educated Malawians nurtured the symbolic legacy of the Chilembwe Uprising into a rallying cry for eventual self-governance and independence from Britain. His name and the sacrifices of 1915 were reclaimed as a point of nationalist pride despite colonial efforts to expunge it. When Malawi did finally achieved independence in 1964 after Chilembwe's uprising had helped pave the way, his role as a founding father was properly recognized. Streets and structures now bear his name, while the date January 15th marks a national public holiday enshrining his legacy as a catalyst for liberation.

More broadly, Chilembwe is remembered as a pioneering African intellectual turned revolutionary whose righteous defiance on that fateful January 1915 evening set an example of bold anti-colonial insurrection inspired by the prophetic ideals of freedom, dignity and autonomy for Africans.

While his armed uprising was ultimately crushed, the shooting flames of resistance it ignited could not be so easily extinguished; burning defiantly until colonial oppression itself was overthrown in Malawi and across the continent. In this light, Chilembwe and his martyrs stand as powerful emblematic figures. Not just for their open revolt, but as early vanguards in the long struggle against imperial subjugation, dispossession and racism that shaped the birth of modern African nationalism in the 20th century.

- Accomplices of Rev John Chilmbwe in the uprising of 1915 being led to their hanging.

Alwy M. Jones

The Massacre That Ignited Mozambique's Liberation Struggle

On June 16th 1960, the village of Mueda in northern Mozambique became the blood soaked crucible catalyzing the Southeast African nation's protracted war for independence from Portuguese colonial rule. Over the course of that fateful day, hundreds of Mozambicans were massacred by Portuguese military forces and colonial militias during a violent crackdown on an organized strike and protests.

While the precise death toll remains disputed, credible estimates suggest at least 1,000 Mozambican civilians and workers were killed in Mueda during the indiscriminate carnage. Homes were looted and burned, while women and children fell victim to the hail of gunfire and mortar shelling.

For the people of Mueda and across Mozambique, June 16th came to be seared into the national consciousness; a day representing the ultimate moral bankruptcy of the Portuguese Estado Novo regime's iron-fisted attempts to preserve its African empire through racist violence and terror.

The origins of the Mueda Massacre traced back to a simmering labor strike by dockworkers of the Muslim Muedane ethnic group employed at the local Mozambique Cotton Company. Grievances over poor working conditions and discrimination escalated into wider protests joined by other Muedane villagers, who marched on colonial government offices that morning demonstrating for basic rights.

According to survivors' accounts, the situation quickly spiraled out of control when Portuguese soldiers and militant Catholic settlers attempted to violently disperse the largely peaceful crowds outside an administrative post. Gunfire erupted, mass panic ensued, and before long Mueda descended into a killing zone. Indiscriminate shelling into residential areas exacted a horrific toll on civilians.

In the massacre's direct aftermath, the Portuguese launched a harsh retaliatory crackdown codenamed Operation Rude Carving involving mass arrests, detention camps, and collective punishments designed to terrorize the Mozambican populace into submission. An eerie silence and media blackout was enforced as military troops consolidated control over the region.

However, rather than stamp out resistance once and for all, the savagery in Mueda backfired spectacularly for the colonial regime. News of the massacre and its civilian casualties reverberated across Mozambique, igniting widespread outrage and swelling the ranks of nationalist groups like FRELIMO determined to claim independence from Portugal through open insurrection.

After the Mueda Massacre, all hope for a negotiated transition to self-governance dissipated as FRELIMO took up arms and launched its guerilla campaign igniting the Mozambican War of Independence in

1964 that would ultimately bleed the Portuguese Army after over a decade of bitter fighting.

Within Mozambique itself, Mueda left a legacy of multi-generational trauma akin to the impact of other colonial-era atrocities like the Amritsar Massacre in India or Sharpeville in South Africa. With entire families dead, villages and communities were torn asunder by the loss of life and violence.

The massacre sites themselves were left as haunted open wounds dotting the landscape, while camps and execution grounds emerged as Calvary sites of death and torture by Portuguese forces seeking to extinguish dissent by any means during the subsequent liberation war.

In the modern era, the Mueda Massacre has been officially commemorated as a national Martyrs' Day in Mozambique since 1976. A large monument complex and museum were constructed at the massacre site to properly memorialize the hundreds gunned down for the cause of independence.

Yet after decades of historiographical silence and revisionism by the former colonial powers, a fuller reckoning over the atrocities committed during Portugal's endgame in Africa has remained a fraught, unresolved legacy for all sides to address. Full accountability, apologies and restorative justice for the victims of massacres like Mueda remains an open wound.

Regardless, the events of that horrific June day in 1960 galvanized a generation of Mozambicans to the cause of liberation from colonial oppression even at the cost of immense bloodshed, trauma and suffering catalyzed by the authorities' own self-defeating brutality. While massacres like Mueda revealed the moral and ethical bankruptcy of the late Portuguese imperial enterprise, they also ignited an inextinguishable blaze of nationalist resistance that no crackdown could ever truly contain.

Wiriyamu's Ghosts: Mozambique's Unhealed Wound of War

On the morning of July 16th 1972, the village of Wiriyamu in northern Mozambique awoke to sounds of gunfire and terror as Portuguese colonial troops and militia forces launched a scorched earth assault. Over the next two days, a massacre of staggering proportions unfolded leaving hundreds of civilians dead and a brutalized community razed to the ground.

While estimates vary, as many as 600 villagers including women, children and elderly were systematically killed by Portuguese soldiers, often through summary executions, arson and bombardments. An entire generation saw their lives extinguished as Portuguese forces sought retribution for perceived support of the FRELIMO liberation movement then waging its insurgency.

For the ethnic Maconde people of Wiriyamu, the massacre represented an apex of terror unleashed by Portugal's war against Mozambican independence. Far from an isolated incident, the atrocities were part of an orchestrated campaign by colonial troops to strategically decimate and depopulate areas seen as FRELIMO strongholds through mass killings, forced displacements and obliteration of whole villages.

In the months prior, Wiriyamu had been temporarily occupied by guerrilla fighters as they pushed deeper into this region near the borders of Tanzania. This prompted ferocious Portuguese reprisals and determination to create a scorched earth buffer through any means necessary.

And so on that fateful July morning, the colonial forces surrounded the village under the cover of darkness and at dawn unleashed their onslaught. Huts were set ablaze while fleeing villagers were gunned down methodically. Even a recently built hospital was bombed despite its protected status under laws of warfare.

The massacres raged over two days until Wiriyamu lay utterly destroyed, its streets and farmlands strewn with the dead. Those not killed outright were displaced across the countryside. As one of the worst single atrocities of the Mozambican war, Wiriyamu made international headlines and drew global condemnations over its barbarity.

While Portugal initially denied the massacre took place, irrefutable evidence soon emerged including testimonies from aid workers and journalists as well as discovered military communiques explicitly detailing plans to extinguish the "anti-Portuguese population" of Wiriyamu.

In the aftermath, a swath of northern Mozambique was declared in a permanent state of terror by FRELIMO. The independence struggle only escalated in intensity and scope as the lines between civilians and combatants blurred for the Portuguese.

When Mozambique did finally achieve its hard-fought liberation in 1975, the wounds of Wiriyamu remained unhealed and haunting. Many of the displaced survivors formed a permanent "Village of Widows" refugee community, unwilling to return to their decimated homeland.

Today, over 50 years since the massacre, Wiriyamu remains an open trauma for the Mozambican nation still struggling with issues of reconciliation and closure from its bitter war of independence.

While the village was eventually rebuilt and repopulated after 1975, the memorials and community hauntings still resonate from the massacre's horrors. Each year on July 16th, commemorations are held to honor the dead and surviving victims who endured the Portuguese brutalities at Wiriyamu. Calls for reparations and justice for affected families remain unresolved.

Perhaps most viscerally, the discovered mass graves bulldozed by Portuguese troops proved impossible to fully identify. The remains of hundreds massacred simply became anonymous bones intermingled in the blood-soaked soil they tried to defend against colonial domination.

For Mozambique, ensuring the massacred civilians of Wiriyamu did not die in complete anonymity remains an open challenge on the road toward historical accountability and reconciliation. Only by fully reckoning with such harrowing chapters can a nation truly heal from the deep, persistent wounds of its violent independence struggle against oppressive colonial rule.

Alwy M. Jones

Confronting Germany's Colonial Genocide

Between 1884 and 1915, the frontier territories of German South-West Africa bore witness to one of the earliest campaigns of genocide perpetrated against indigenous populations in the modern colonial era. Over this span, the German Empire's rapacious pursuit of conquest and racial superiority in Africa directly caused the decimation of the Nama and Herero ethnic groups through a ruthless combination of orchestrated massacres, forced labor, concentration camps, and deprivation tactics.

The initial sparks were lit in 1884 when Berlin formally established the territory as an overseas imperial possession called German South-West Africa. Within the first decade, widespread resentment built among the Nama and Herero peoples as their ancestral lands and resources were systematically seized and exploited. Clashes with German "Schutztruppe" troops over grazing rights and sovereignty escalated tensions dramatically.

In January 1904, open rebellion erupted as Herero militants launched attacks on German colonial settlements in a bid to drive the occupying forces out. In retaliation, the notorious German commander Lothar von Trotha enacted his policy of exterminating the Herero nation through total warfare; unleashing his troops in a scorched earth campaign across the central Namibian territories.

What followed were a series of massacres, settlement bombings, forced marches into the desert without provisions, mass summary executions of men, women and children, and the first use of concentration camps in the 20th century to complete the genocidal campaign. Poisoning of wells and other deprivation tactics accelerated the death toll.

"The nation has . . . to defend itself," declared von Trotha in justifying his brutal orders. "I will annihilate the revolting tribes with rivers of blood. Within the German boundaries, every Herero, whether found armed or defenseless, will be executed."

By 1905, organized Herero resistance had been crushed through such merciless methods. But German troops also turned on rebelling Nama groups that same year, unleashing similar massacres, population transfers and extermination camps to complete their subjugation.

Exact figures are still debated, but historians suggest over 65,000 Herero; 60% of their total population perished through the Germans' calculated campaign. Another 10,000 Nama people, around half their number, were also wiped out through killings and deprivations in the concentration camp network.

 First-hand accounts chronicled the Germans' industrial-scale killings and erasure of these indigenous cultures, describing the desert strewn with bodies and piles of bleached skulls collected as battlefield trophies. Entire family lineages and ancestral knowledge was exterminated through both direct violence and the torturous conditions in the camps.

For the Herero and Nama survivors driven into exile or displaced from their ravaged homelands, the collective trauma would reverberate across generations through poverty, social disruption and ongoing dispossession of their lands from foreign settlers.

While the German Empire made cynical attempts to downplay or deny the genocidal events, international outcry and missionary accounts gradually exposed the truth of the coordinated massacres. However, Germany refused to formally apologize or issue reparations at the time, cementing the atrocities as one of the 20th century's earliest and most overlooked genocides.

It was only in 2004 that a century after the Herero massacres began that the German government finally acknowledged and issued an official apology for the "genocidal war of extermination" waged by its colonial forefathers. Namibia and NGOs continue actively campaigning for restorative justice and historical reparations to finally close this agonizing chapter.

In the modern day, the dark legacies of this first genocide of the 1900s still haunt the Namibian national psyche through intergenerational trauma, land ownership struggles between the government and ethnic groups, and active preservation of the

Herero and Nama cultures that were once so nearly destroyed.

Memorials, museums and massacre sites now dot the desert landscapes of central Namibia with grim reminders of the tens of thousands of civilian lives obliterated over colonial greed and notions of racial hierarchies. Germany's undeniable transgressions in systematically hunting, massacring and driving indigenous groups to extinction helped set the stage for 20th century's subsequent atrocities.

Namibia's experience stands as a haunting premonition of the disastrous consequences when European colonial ambition combined with pseudo-scientific racism allowed dehumanization and mass violence to achieve their poisonous ends. While the Herero and Nama cultures still endure in spite of those genocidal efforts, the Namibian nation and global consciousness must continue reckoning with the traumatic shadows of this overlooked chapter in humanity's ultimate descent into industrialized genocide during the colonial age.

Prisoners from the Herero and Nama tribes during the 1904-1908 war against Germany.

Alwy M. Jones

Nigeria's Labor Awakening Born in Blood

On November 18th 1949, a brutal crackdown by colonial police forces on striking Nigerian miners and their families in the remote Iva Valley marked a pivotal, often overlooked, chapter in the nation's struggle for workers' rights and eventual independence from British rule.

At the Iva Valley coal mines, nearly 1,000 members of the Workers Union had been engaged in protests and non-violent sit-ins for several weeks demanding better wages and living conditions from the British management. Tensions had steadily escalated as the strikes intensified, culminating in a final confrontation on that fateful November day.

What exactly transpired at the Iva Valley mines remains disputed between colonial authorities' accounts and oral histories from witnesses. But most narratives agree that when police reinforcements arrived by train to break up the striking workers' blockades, chaos and gunfire soon erupted.

British officials claimed the miners first instigated violence by stoning officers. However, many worker testimonies allege police opened fire indiscriminately after protesters refused to disperse, gunning down scores of unarmed men, women and children.

When the smoke finally cleared, the death toll from the massacre stood at anywhere between 20 (the colonial record) and 70 according to workers' representatives, with untold numbers more injured and arrested. Entire families lost relatives in the sudden hail of bullets and tear gas that day.

In the massacre's immediate aftermath, colonial authorities swiftly cracked down on dissent and labor organizing, enacting curfews, arrests and other repressive measures to reassert control and discourage any further unrest from spreading. Disturbances were officially blamed on "irresponsible elements."

However, the heavy-handed violence at Iva Valley had the opposite effect; catalyzing rather than deterring Nigeria's growing independence movement coalescing within its labor unions, civil societies, and educated urban circles.

Outrage over the massacre helped propel the previously marginalized Nigerian labor unions into the forefront as a political force demanding an end to imperial subjugation and economic exploitation. It set the stage for figures like Michael Imoudu to rise as mobilizing voices rallying strikers, marchers and civil disobedience campaigns.

Over the coming years, the unaddressed grievances underlying the Iva Valley killings only intensified nationalist calls for self-determination and sovereignty as Nigeria's journey to independence after WWII accelerated. By 1960, the protest movements and labor activism sparked by Iva Valley had achieved their ultimate goals as Africa's most populous nation finally secured independence from Britain.

In this light, while Iva Valley represented a tragic nadir of British repression and overreaction against colonial Nigeria's labor movements, it also proved to be the necessary catalyst awakening the populace to the brutality and injustice underpinning imperial rule. The massacre's martyrs did not die in vain.

While modern Nigeria has grappled with its own challenges of governance and unrest in recent decades, the solemn commemorations of the Iva Valley Massacre each November 18th remain poignant reminders of the foundational blood, sweat and tears that paved its path to sovereignty.

And more broadly, the events of 1949 stand as one of the seminal chapters highlighting how colonial labor uprisings and violent reprisals catalyzed the flowering of anti-imperial nationalist movements across Africa in the 20th century's twilight era of European rule. Out of these massacres, charismatic organizers and visions of independence were born reflecting the common struggles of subjugated peoples demanding self-determination at any cost.

Alwy M. Jones

Reckoning with Sao Tome's Searing Legacy of Colonial Massacre

On the morning of February 3rd, 1953, the sleepy agricultural village of Batepa on the island of Sao Tome awoke to unimaginable horror and bloodshed at the hands of Portuguese colonial forces and their allied militia units. Over the course of a single day, vengeful troops indiscriminately massacred hundreds of civilians engaged in non-violent protests marking one of the darkest chapters in the history of Portugal's island colony.

The massacre's origins traced back to brewing resentment among Sao Tome's native contract workers over the exploitative labor conditions enforced on Portuguese-owned cocoa and coffee plantations. In January 1953, peaceful strikes and marches had escalated calling for wage increases and better treatment.

However, colonial administrators viewed this labor defiance as sedition that needed to be crushed. As protests swelled in late January onto plantations like Roça Sundy, the infamous Portuguese Lt. Colonel Carlos Deslandes was dispatched to Batepa with overwhelming military force to forcibly restore productivity and obedience by any means necessary.

On February 3rd, when Deslandes' troops encountered local protestors gathered in Batepa's Cidra plantation, a brief scuffle broke out that provided the flashpoint for carnage. By many accounts, Portuguese troops simply opened fire indiscriminately into crowds of confused civilians, the bulk of whom were unarmed plantation workers alongside some of their family members.

What followed were hours of an almost industrialized slaughter as Deslandes directed relentless mortar, artillery and rifle fire into Batepa's villages. Colonial troops and militia gunmen hunted down fleeing residents and executed them in masses. Those seeking sanctuary in homes or churches found no protection from the onslaught.

According to survivor testimonies compiled decades later, the screams and wails of the wounded and dying mingled with the pungent smoke and stench of blood as colonists' long-simmering racist contempt was unleashed in the most horrific fashion imaginable.

"It was like the fires of hell," an elderly survivor recalled in 2010. "Our pleas for mercy were answered only with more bullets, grenades and torched huts..."

By nightfall, the coastal village and surrounding farms lay in smoldering ruin as the shooting finally subsided. Official Portuguese tallies listed just 36 deaths, while Catholic missionaries estimated over 700 murdered in Batepa by Deslandes' rampage. Mass graves were unceremoniously dug to dispose of the bodies of slain innocents.

In the aftermath, martial law was imposed across Sao Tome, arrests spiked, and a chilling silence fell over the archipelago as news of the massacre's brutality seeped out through international pressures and whistleblowers. Portugal vehemently denied any wrongdoing, claiming it had simply quelled a dangerous revolt of "savages."

However, the sheer depravity of the Batepa bloodbath galvanized global backlash against Portuguese colonialism and its hypocrisy toward supposed "civilizing" missions in Africa. It became emblematic of Europe's declining empires resorting to barbarous violence and scorched earth tactics against indigenous populations in their death throes.

Within Sao Tome, Batepa forged itself into the national psyche as an open, gaping wound never allowed to fully heal by the colonial censorship and occupation that persisted for another two decades until independence in 1975. In this vacuum, whispered oral histories and forbidden songs memorialized the massacre's victims and their sacrifices.

Today, Batepa remains enshrined in Sao Tomean memorials and cultural commemorations held each February as a stark reminder of the heavy blood price paid over the long, tortured path to sovereignty. The site itself, known as the "Valle de Sangue" (Valley of Blood), has become a pilgrimage site for mourners and a haunting monument to the hundreds whose very graves and names have long since been obscured by the passage of time.

In many ways, the Batepa Massacre represented the inevitable clash between colonized African labor and dignity versus Europe's commitment to racial subjugation and extractive economic exploitation no matter how extreme the violence deployed.

While smaller in death toll than contemporaneous anti-colonial massacres like those in Kenya and Algeria, Batepa was no less emblematic of the existential struggles playing out across the continent. Indigenous societies that had endured centuries of oppressive foreign domination were making a firm stand that only their independence from imperial rule remained acceptable even at the cost of gruesome retaliation from the entrenched colonial powers.

Through this harrowing crucible, figures like Batepa would become sacrosanct within individual nations' liberation movements and broader Pan-African consciousness. The bloodied grounds represented a collective sacrifice to the cause of expelling racist imperial regimes and charting Africa's own sovereign destinies.

However, for Sao Tome and Principe, Batepa also still epitomizes the incalculable trauma that festered for decades erasing entire lineages and cultural memory while displacement and silence allowed the systemic injustices to fester. Even now, discussions of truth and reconciliation persist over Portugal's culpability, the incomplete historical record, and whether restorative justice for the massacres' descendants can ever be rendered beyond remembrance.

Above all, the martyrs of Batepa remain an open reminder of the cruelties Europeans inflicted on Africans over the colonial era, and the perseverance of the human spirit to still fight for freedom, dignity and self-determination despite overwhelming oppression. Their loss shaped a nation, even if their individual names are now obscured by history and time's indifference.

Alwy M. Jones

Senegal's Disillusionment with the Colonial Myth

On the morning of November 30th 1944, the sleepy village of Thiaroye near Dakar, Senegal became the site of one of the most horrific massacres perpetrated against African colonial troops by European occupiers. Over the span of just a few fateful hours, French officers and gendarmes gunned down hundreds of their own demobilized West African infantry in a frenzy of violence that shattered any remaining myths of a benevolent or mutually sacrificing colonial hierarchy.

The origins of the tragedy can be traced to the marshaling of thousands of Senegalese tirailleurs serving in the French West African colonies to provide infantry in the European and North African theaters against the Axis powers. These largely Africans answered the call to arms to fight fascism under the idealistic goal of receiving equal rights and payback terms as their white French compatriots.

However, by late 1944 as the war drew to a close in Europe, festering grievances had been building among the tirailleurs over rampant discrimination, unequal living conditions, and especially discrepancies in pay and pension packages promised if they were demobilized versus their white metropolitan counterparts. Protests and acts of insubordination in Senegal reflected the growing defiance.

In response, the French military command opted to employ brute force in an attempt to swiftly crush any potential "mutiny" before broader unrest could spread. On November 30th, French gendarmes surrounded camps containing thousands of tirailleurs awaiting demobilization transit near the village of Thiaroye.

Contemporary accounts describe how initially peaceful protests by African soldiers quickly descended into chaos as gendarmes inexplicably opened fire into the crowds after facing taunts and rocks. Rather than de-escalate, French officers on the scene doubled down calling in artillery bombardments and armored vehicles to indiscriminately attack the tirailleurs. A massacre lasting nearly an entire day ensued before colonial reinforcement regained control.

In the massacre's wake, over 300 Senegalese tirailleurs lay dead cut down by the very colonial power they had served. Hundreds more were injured, with dozens later executed by firing squads or jailed. Mass graves were hastily prepared to bury the fallen.

For the people of Senegal and its returning soldiers, the Thiaroye Massacre inflicted a severe crisis of confidence in France's "civilizing" rhetoric and the realities of colonial injustice. How could black African soldiers be so unjustly massacred after sacrificing for the ideals of liberation from tyranny?

France's initial efforts to censor details of the massacre eventually crumbled as irrefutable evidence emerged not just of the bloodshed, but the colonial regime's explicit orders to use lethal force on its own African colonial troops. Promises of equal pensions and back-pay became seen as duplicitous pretexts.

In the short term, these revelations galvanized existing Senegalese independence movements who cited Thiaroye as the ultimate moral indictment of the French empire's racist contradictions on respecting African life and self-determination. Civil disobedience and labor strikes escalated in Dakar.

Even after Senegal's independence was achieved in 1960, the national trauma of Thiaroye remained an open wound for generations of Senegalese to grapple with moving forward. Annual commemorations recalling the massacre became sacred events, while monuments in Dakar honored those cut down for seeking equality.

More broadly, Thiaroye represented an early postwar catalyst for the broader decolonization struggles soon to sweep across French West Africa and beyond. The simmering resentments over colonial oppression and institutionalized racism finally boiled over in bloodshed. Coming on the heels of World War II's carnage and Nazi horrors, the Thiaroye massacre laid bare a harsh reality; that even among the victorious Allied colonial powers, repugnant racial hierarchies enabling mass violence were deeply entrenched.

For Senegal and other emerging independent African nations, Thiaroye martyrs embodied the collective sacrifices made not just in service to others' wars, but in the existential struggle to overthrow the entire colonial system. Their disillusionment with France's hypocrisy fueled a reckoning that took the form of nationalist liberation movements and sundering ties with European imperial centers.

Even today, the commemorations and monuments to Thiaroye ensure the tragedy is never forgotten in Senegal's historical memory. The massacre represents a pivotal inflection point where colonial myths of mutual uplift and sacrifice were irrevocably shattered with echoes of this painful disillusionment still reverberating through the nation's reckoning with its independence origins.

Alwy M. Jones

When Apartheid's Bullets Shattered Illusions

On March 21st 1985, the sprawling Langa Township outside Cape Town became the bloody crucible where South Africa's anti-apartheid struggle was crystallized in all its brutal complexity. Over the span of just a few hours that fateful evening, South African police opened fire on a crowd of protesters, massacring at least 20 people and injuring over 100 more. The victims were overwhelmingly innocent bystanders including elderly residents, students and children.

What became known as the Langa Massacre encapsulated the full horror and injustice of the apartheid regime's willingness to unleash indiscriminate violence to crush even peaceful resistance to its racist ideology of white minority rule. The day's events also propelled the townships into the vanguard of mass defiance, leading inexorably toward the political conflagration soon to engulf all of South Africa just a few years later.

The seeds of the massacre were sown earlier that month as protests and rent strikes swept Langa and other black townships in Cape Town over deteriorating living conditions and resentments against the hated apartheid policies and restrictions on movement. On March 21st, a massive demonstration including students on their way to class assembled at the township's railway station before South African police moved to violently disperse it.

Contemporary witness accounts describe the scenes of terror as police indiscriminately fired tear gas canisters, rubber bullets and then switched to using live ammunition into panicked crowds trying to flee the chaos. Images of police armored vehicles pursuing vulnerable bystanders and children being gunned down as they scrambled for cover soon made international headlines and drew global outrage.

In the immediate aftermath, the true toll of bloodshed became clear, over 60 had perished according to activists' records, including an 18 month old infant. The official police inquiry downplayed the death toll to just over 20. Regardless, Langa's victims were enshrined as the first major township massacre since the Sharpeville killings 25 years prior.

For South Africa's beleaguered anti-apartheid movement, Langa represented an earth shattering wake-up call. Any illusions of the racist regime's willingness to enact meaningful reforms or avoid further lethal crackdowns had been shattered by the indiscriminate carnage visited upon these innocents simply clamoring for basic rights and dignities.

In the aftermath, civil resistance soared in Langa and neighboring townships as the United Democratic Front coalition led protests, rent boycotts and mass funerals for the "Langa martyrs." Violence and clashes with security forces steadily escalated across the Greater Cape Town area into a full-scale rebellion by 1986 that the apartheid government proved increasingly powerless to contain through brute force alone.

Langa proved to be a harbinger and catalyst for the broader mass defiance campaigns that soon engulfed the entire country, eroding any remaining domestic and international credibility of the apartheid system's moral foundations. Nelson Mandela himself drew inspiration from the massacre's victims in his writings while imprisoned, enshrining March 21st as a rallying date for freedom fighters to "render apartheid unworkable."

In a tragic irony, the apartheid regime's determination to ruthlessly crush any flickers of resistance in Langa through overwhelming force only poured gasoline onto long-simmering outrage that soon detonated into an unstoppable conflagration.

Even as the dismantling of formal apartheid policies proceeded in the early 1990s and South Africa's democratic transition began, the wounds left by the Langa massacre never fully healed for the families and communities most impacted. Controversies persisted over the lack of disciplinary action taken against police involved and an overall failure to pursue restorative justice through truth and reconciliation processes.

To this day in Langa, the scene of the massacre remains a haunted space memorialized with public artwork and monuments to the fallen "heroes of the resistance." Annual commemorations feature rallies, marches and the honoring of eyewitness accounts to ensure the tragic violence of March 21st, 1985 never fades from the national consciousness.

The ripple effects still resonate through South African society over how such a catalyzing atrocity born of the apartheid state's desperation to preserve minority rule at any cost laid bare the rot at the system's core and galvanized popular resistance into an inextinguishable moral force. From Langa's blood-soaked streets also emerged the vanguards of a new generation carrying the torch of the anti-apartheid struggle who within their lifetime would live to see the construction of a new, democratic and multi-racial South Africa.

Coffins of the Langa Massacre's victims.

Alwy M. Jones

The Apartheid Drug Scandal: Mind Control Through Substance Abuse

During the darkest days of apartheid rule in South Africa, disturbing reports have surfaced about the regime's security forces utilizing drugs like Mandrax (methaqualone) and ecstasy as tools of oppression and control. These allegations reveal a sinister strategy that not only devastated lives but undermined entire communities.

Mandrax, a sedative and hypnotic substance, was widely abused in South Africa's townships in the 1970s and 1980s. However, according to whistle-blowers and former operatives, the apartheid government deliberately fueled this drug crisis by flooding black neighborhoods with Mandrax, rendering residents docile and easier to control.

Beyond just distributing the drug, there are chilling accounts of security forces directly administering Mandrax and other substances to detainees during interrogations. The aim was to weaken their resistance and make them more compliant to harsh questioning and even torture.

In the later years of apartheid rule in the 1980s, ecstasy allegedly became another drug of choice for disrupting anti-government activities. The euphoric and disorienting effects of this substance were reportedly exploited to dampen the spirits of activists and sow confusion within the resistance movement.

The long-term impacts of this chemically enforced oppression are still being felt today throughout South Africa's communities. Rampant substance abuse, fractured families, and mental health issues are just some of the lingering side effects.

Moreover, despite the new democratic regime's efforts at securing justice, the full truth about the apartheid regime's drug operations may never come to light, as records were likely destroyed and operatives granted amnesty for their crimes.

As South Africa continues to grapple with its scars of the past, the alleged weaponing of drugs like Mandrax and ecstasy by the former security forces stands as one of the most unnerving and unforgivable tactics of the apartheid system's desperate attempt to cling to power.

Alwy M. Jones

How Sharpeville Shook Apartheid's Foundations

On a fateful day in 1960, this modest township outside Vereeniging became immortalized as the site of one of the most horrific massacres in South Africa's turbulent struggle against apartheid. When peaceful protesters defying the regime's hated pass laws were met with lethal force from police on March 21st, the tragic events of the Sharpeville Massacre sent shockwaves throughout the country and the world.

It was supposed to be a non-violent demonstration, organized by a small group affiliated with the Pan Africanist Congress (PAC). Their target was the local police station, where they intended to turn themselves in for not carrying the reviled passbooks that codified the racist system's draconian controls on black movement and rights.

But as the numbers swelled into the thousands, the peaceful scene devolved into chaos. Police reinforcements arrived, quickly becoming overwhelmed by the sheer size of the demonstration. While the circumstances remain hotly debated, the first shots rang out from the police lines around 1pm.

When the smoke cleared, the official death toll stood at 69 killed and over 180 wounded, one of the worst single incidents of civilian massacre in modern South African history. Among the dozens left lifeless in Sharpeville's dusty streets were 8 women and 10 children.

News of the savage crackdown ignited immediate outrage both domestically and around the globe. Protests and riots erupted nationwide as the African National Congress (ANC) and other groups declared a stay-at-home strike. The international community reacted with disgust, levying sanctions and boycotts on the apartheid regime.

For the ANC's figurehead Nelson Mandela, Sharpeville marked a pivotal turning point. "The massacre dissipated any notion of peaceful protest being met with anything but merciless brutality," he wrote years later. "It steeled our resolve to pursue armed struggle as the only remaining path to liberation."

Indeed, within months, Mandela had established ANC's armed wing, ushering in a new era of guerilla warfare, sabotage, and escalating bloodshed between the government and its black opposition. Sharpeville also galvanized global support and solidarity for the anti-apartheid cause. In 1966, the United Nations established March 21st as the annual International Day for the Elimination of Racial Discrimination in solemn remembrance of the massacre's victims.

Alwy M. Jones

The Haunting Legacy of the Maji Maji Massacres

More than a century ago, this corner of Africa witnessed unfathomable bloodshed and suffering during the Maji Maji Rebellion against German colonial rule. Sparked by a spiritual leaders' calls to use traditional charms and rituals to repel the colonists' bullets, the uprising by local ethnic groups quickly grew into a widespread revolt. However, the German forces' superior weaponry crushed the rebellion through a ruthless campaign of massacres, hangings, and a scorched earth policy that left the lands depopulated.

Today, the physical and psychological scars from those dark years remain embedded in the cultural fabric of communities like the Ngoni. It's estimated that the German brutality and famine caused by the conflict killed at least 300,000 people, over a third of the entire Ngoni population at the time.

This collective generational trauma has manifested in very real ways. Traditional rituals and songs evoking the massacres keep the horrific memories alive. Mental health issues like depression, anxiety and substance abuse remain stubborn problems. And with so many men killed, gender imbalances still persist to this day.

In the village of Kitanda, an unassuming tree bears carved crosses marking one of the mass grave sites from the rebellion era.

There are efforts to officially memorialize the Maji Maji tragedy as a profound turning point that accelerated the demise of German East Africa and catalyzed early Tanzanian nationalist sentiments. A museum in Dar es Salaam documents the history through artifacts and first-hand accounts.

However, in the rural communities where so much blood soaked the earth, the massacres remain an open wound fueling calls to preserve this haunting past.

Togo's Pya-Hodo Massacre

Over 65 years ago, this small West African nation was rocked by one of the darkest chapters of its struggle for independence from French colonial rule. The Pya-Hodo Massacre of June 21st, 1957 saw French forces unleash indiscriminate violence that left dozens of Togolese civilians dead and hundreds more injured. While the horrific event helped catalyze the independence movement, its deep wounds have never fully healed.

The seeds were planted in 1956 when the pro-independence Comite de l'Union Togolaise (CUT) party swept regional elections, threatening French colonial control. Hardline French administrators like Governor Georges Mauge aimed to suppress the rising nationalist tide through brute force if necessary.

On that fateful June day in 1957, a CUT political rally of several thousand was taking place in the village of Pya-Hodo, about 30 miles north of the capital Lome. Tensions were already high following riots and clashes earlier that year. As the crowd swelled with locals and party supporters, French military units surrounded the area.

The French opened fire with machine guns and tossed grenades directly into the crowd. It was indiscriminate slaughter of the old, women, children cut down in the hail of bullets.

Estimates vary on the final death toll, with French authorities at the time admitting to only a handful of fatalities while Togolese independence groups have put the number as high as 500 massacred. Hundreds more were injured and arrested. It was a clearly calculated effort by the French to make a brutal example and to brutally crush the desire for liberation through sheer violence and state terror. In their vain attempt to decapitate our nationalist movement, they instead created patriotic martyrs whose blood inspired generations of resistance.

Indeed, in the aftermath of the Pya-Hodo Massacre, the CUT's independence struggle gained renewed vigor and international sympathy. After nearly a decade more of civil unrest and French concessions, Togo finally achieved independence on April 27th, 1960 with the CUT's Sylvanus Olympio assuming power as the first president.

However, the traumatic legacy of Pya-Hodo still casts a long shadow. Annual commemorations honor those slain with traditional songs and ceremonies. Community leaders bemoan how the event destabilized the social and economic fabric through displacement and animosity towards French nationals who remained. Most significantly, some Togolese claim the seeds of the country's eventual descent into military coups and political unrest in the post-colonial era can be traced to the unaddressed trauma of the 1957 massacre. As Togo continues its halting march towards democracy today, the ghosts of Pya-Hodo remain a solemn reminder of both the monumental sacrifice made for freedom, and the work still left in healing its deep-rooted wounds.

Zimbabwe's Darkest Stain

In this remote village in northeastern Zimbabwe, the scars from one of the most brutal atrocities of the Rhodesian Bush War remain raw decades later. On August 5th, 1976, Rhodesian security forces carried out a cold-blooded massacre of civilian men, women and children that shocked the world and helped galvanize international support for the liberation struggle.

It was the height of the bitter conflict between the white minority government of Rhodesia and the Black Nationalist guerilla forces fighting for majority rule and independence. The area around Nyadzonia had become a hotbed of support for Robert Mugabe's ZANU militant wing.

Determined to cut off the rebels from their civilian supporters, Rhodesian troops descended on Nyadzonia in the pre-dawn hours, surrounding the sleeping village under the cover of darkness.

What followed was a merciless slaughter of the defenseless villagers; the precise death toll remains unknown to this day. Hundreds were undoubtedly gunned down in cold blood that morning based on eyewitness accounts. Many others were burned alive as soldiers set huts and buildings ablaze.

Aside from the sheer brutality, what made the Nyadzonia Massacre so infamous was the cold calculation behind it. Clearly outlined in the Rhodesian military's counterinsurgency doctrine, the massive loss of civilian life was a deliberate tactic to terrorize and deprive rebel forces of their civilian support base.

Indeed, news of the massacre sparked immediate outrage and condemnation across the continent and globe. Newly independent African nations led by Mozambique rallied further support and material aid for the Zimbabwean guerillas. The United Nations imposed further sanctions, isolating Rhodesia as an international pariah.

While the full details remain clouded by time and biased accounts, the Nyadzonia Massacre undeniably became a galvanizing catalyst in the liberation struggle's ultimate success. Just four years later in 1980, the country achieved majority rule and independence, reborn as Zimbabwe under Robert Mugabe's leadership.

However, the open wound of Nyadzonia still festers for many. A modest stone memorial now stands in the village bearing the names of the known dead. But reminders are everywhere of the burned-out ruins of homesteads, tales of the missing passed through generations.

Yet even today, some alleged perpetrators have escaped accountability. After the transition to majority rule, most Rhodesian forces were granted amnesty in the name of unity and reconciliation.

Alwy M. Jones

Unearthing the Chimoio Massacre

In this sleepy town near the Zimbabwean border, few outward signs remain of one of the most brutal and underreported atrocities committed during the long conflicts that bled across the region in the 1970s. But for those who survived the Chimoio Massacre of November 1977, the trauma remains as fresh as an open wound.

At the time, Chimoio housed a major rear camp and base for Robert Mugabe's ZANU guerilla forces fighting for majority rule in what was then Rhodesia. Despite Mozambique's post-colonial government allowing the rebels sanctuary on their soil, Rhodesian military commanders were determined to destroy this perceived safe haven through whatever means necessary.

Under the cover of night on November 23rd, a highly trained force of over 600 Rhodesian troops, along with helicopter gunships, launched a cross-border raid deep into Mozambique. Their target: the dense cluster of huts housing thousands of ZANU fighters, refugees, and their families in Chimoio.

What followed was a massacre of staggering proportions. Caught completely unawares, the camp was defenseless against the onslaught of attackers unleashing a withering combination of artillery, aerial bombardment, and infantry sweeps that left few alive.

While difficult to substantiate given the remote location's constraints, estimates from aid workers and journalists who reached Chimoio in the aftermath put the death toll at least 5,000 dead, with thousands more injured. Entire families were simply wiped out in the onslaught without discrimination.

Though the camp itself harbored combatants, the overwhelming majority of victims were unarmed civilians; women, children, and the elderly who suffered a gruesome fate simply from being in the line of fire. Those who managed to flee into the surrounding forests faced future deprivation from the loss of food stores, supplies, and medical facilities.

The Rhodesian forces proclaimed the surprise attack a tactical success in disrupting the ZANU operations and supply lines. But for the world at large, the sheer scale of civilian casualties at Chimoio was a searing indictment of the white minority regime's desperation and depravity.

Indeed, in the decades since, memorializing those who perished at Chimoio has remained fraught, seen by some as a necessary tragedy in the cause of overthrowing Rhodesian rule, while others still grapple with how so many innocents were sacrificed.

A modest plaque sits on a hillside commemorating the date of the massacre, but listing no further details. Down an overgrown road, the outlines of mass grave trenches remain, blanketed by the encroaching foliage of the tropical forests.

Alwy M. Jones

Confronting the Lingering Wounds of the 1908 Massacre

Over a century ago, this unassuming city became the epicenter of an eruption of racial violence so heinous, it still casts a long shadow felt to this day. The Springfield Massacre of August 1908 saw armed white mobs brutally attack and kill dozens of African American residents in a nauseating purge of hate.

The tragic chain of events began with a rally held by opponents of the planned relocation of a Black businessman's construction material yard into a white neighborhood. The spiraling unrest finally boiled over on August 14th after the alleged assault of a white man was used as pretext by thousands of angry whites to descend on the Black community. Armed whites flooded onto our streets, shooting and beating any Negro in sight.

By the time the bloodshed finally ended on August 16th, the official death toll listed 9 African American fatalities, but eyewitnesses and historians agree the number was much higher, with scores more injured. The white mob laid waste to prosperous Black businesses on Trade Street, burned entire city blocks of homes, and assaulted residents indiscriminately.

As word spread nationwide of the horrors gripping Springfield, condemnations poured in from Black leaders like W.E.B. Du Bois and Ida B. Wells. A mass exodus of hundreds of terrified Black families fleeing for safety only deepened the city's racial divides.

In the massacre's immediate aftermath, efforts to reform police procedures and rebuild did little to address the long-festering injustices. Businesses struggled as the most affluent Blacks abandoned Springfield for good. And despite indictments against over 100 riot participants, an incumbent system of discriminatory laws ensured only one white man received cursory punishment. The message was clear Black lives, livelihoods, and aspirations for equality amounted to nothing.

NEGRO IS A MENACE

DANGEROUS WITH BALLOT, SAYS GRIGGS OF GEORGIA.

SHOULD BE DEPRIVED OF IT

WHITE CONTROL IN SOUTH ABSOLUTELY NECESSARY.

Prediction Made of a Terrible Race War if Conditions Do Not Change—Can Be No Amalgamation.

- Nebraska State Journal 1908

Alwy M. Jones

An Open Wound on the Piney Woods

On a sweltering July day in 1910, this small, predominantly Black community in East Texas' Piney Woods region was shattered by an outburst of racial violence so brutal, its legacy still haunts the area over a century later.

What started as a dispute between a white man and a Black teenager quickly devolved into an all-out racial massacre, with armed white mobs from across the region descending on Slocum. Over the course of several nights of terror, homes and businesses were torched, innocents were murdered indiscriminately, and the entire African American population was essentially run out of town.

While the exact death toll remains unknown due to the chaos and purposeful obfuscation of records, credible estimates from witnesses and historians put the number of Black fatalities at least 200, earning it a gruesome place in history as potentially one of the deadliest racial injustices of the early 20th century. Babies were bayoneted, women assaulted in broad daylight; it was nothing short of ethnic cleansing of the most brutal and heinous variety.

What is certain is that in the massacre's immediate aftermath, the thriving Black community of Slocum was utterly decimated. Properties and livelihoods built by generations were erased overnight amidst the climate of pure terror. Hundreds fled into the woods and sheltered with Native American tribes for safety.

Those who remained saw their population dwindle away from both violence and forced re-locations over subsequent decades until the original township ceased to exist.

More damning however, was the utter failure and apparent complicity of state authorities at all levels to intervene and prevent the atrocity or even mete out justice in its aftermath. Local law enforcement did nothing to stop the onslaught of mobs or protect innocent lives. The governor at the time downplayed the crisis, and criminal charges were simply never pursued against the instigators.

Indeed, in the decades since 1910, Slocum has remained an open wound for the few remaining descendants of survivors scattered to the wind across the Lone Star State with roots brutally severed. While efforts have been made to erect historical markers and memorials in recent years, many feel true reconciliation remains elusive without fully addressing the past atrocities on an institutional level.

EIGHTEEN NEGROES KILLED BY WHITES

Race War at Slocum, Texas---All Saloons Closed and State Troops Marching to the Scene

PALESTINE, Texas, July 30.—At least eighteen negroes were killed in a racial clash in the extreme eastern section of Anderson county last night and today, the culmination of an enmity between the races brewing for several weeks.

Less conservative reports place the total fatalities at between thirty and forty. It was also reported that several white men were either killed or wounded, but all rumors as to casualties among the whites have met an authoritative denial.

- Headline and lead paragraph in The Salt Lake Herald-Republican of July 31st 1910

Alwy M. Jones

The Enduring Legacy of the Ludlow Massacre

More than a century ago, this small coal mining colony became seared into the American consciousness as the site of one of the most notorious labor massacres in U.S. history. On April 20th 1914, a day etched in tragic infamy, state militia forces attacked a tent colony of striking coal miners and their families in a conflict that would ultimately claim dozens of lives, many of them innocent women and children.

The events that unfolded in Ludlow that spring were the bloody climax of escalating tensions in Colorado's coalfields, where miners had been engaged in a hard-fought strike against coal operators in the notoriously brutal industry. Protesting abysmal wages and living conditions, the workers had been forced to resign from company housing, erecting tent camps where whole families took up residence as the labor standoff dragged into the winter.

It was in one of these colonies, organized under the United Mine Workers union in Ludlow, where state and company forces amassed in preparation for an assault intended to dislodge the striking workers. In the early morning darkness of April 20th, machine gun fire from militia camps rained down on the tents, indiscriminately cutting down those within. While the full details remain contested over a century later with company and state records lost or destroyed, modern historians estimate the final death toll was at least 199, including many women and children taking shelter in the tents. Roughly a dozen more perished afterwards from their wounds. What is indisputable is that Ludlow instantly became a searing indictment of American industrialists' brutality toward immigrant workers and labor rights. John D. Rockefeller Jr., whose family had ownership stakes in Colorado's coalfields, was lambasted for insisting the massacre was inexcusable even if provoked. The strikers' leader, Louis Tikas, became a national hero for the labor movement while surviving miners' family members like Maria Zaharias toured the country bearing witness to the unthinkable atrocities of April 20th. While an official White House mediation enforced a return to work after the summer, public outcry over the Ludlow Massacre proved a watershed moment in galvanizing government reforms like child labor laws and collective bargaining provisions. Multiple investigations and lawsuits uncovered shocking details of widespread miner exploitation, blacklisting practices, and corrupted state forces' complicity with coal operators.

But in Ludlow itself, the scars have proven indelible. The former tent colony remains preserved, its rusted tent poles and shattered pit mines offering mute testimony. More striking is the Ludlow Monument, or "Miners' Memorial." Inlaid with inscriptions detailing the tragedy, its towering statue depicts an emaciated miner bearing a cruelly ironic message: "Those terrible creatures were once as you."

Alwy M. Jones

A Solemn Reckoning in the Wake of the Porvenir Massacre

Over a century ago, this humble ranch settlement near the Mexico border bore witness to one of the most horrific and little-known episodes of racial violence in the tumultuous years surrounding the Mexican Revolution and World War I.

On the night of January 28th 1918, a state-sanctioned vigilante force comprised of Texas Rangers, U.S. cavalrymen, and local ranchers descended on the village of Porvenir with a shocking directive to execute every man in sight over the age of 16. Their perceived crime? Allegedly sheltering Mexican rebels and bandits.

What unfolded was a massacre of staggering inhumanity. From eyewitness accounts passed through generations, the women and children of Porvenir were firstly forced out of their homes into the freezing night air at gunpoint. Then over several hours, the men and teenage boys were systematically rounded up, brought into the village center, and summarily executed by firing squads in cold blood.

The official death toll over 30 according to sources, there is no uncertainty about how indiscriminately the victims were slaughtered, guilty or innocent. No trials or due process ever took place.

In the massacre's wake, the devastated families were forcibly exiled from Porvenir, leaving behind livestock, land and possessions as they fled south across the nearby Rio Grande into Mexico. For years and generations, survivors existed as displaced refugees scattered across border towns before attempting to rebuild their lives.

Yet despite such a grotesque injustice, those culpable were never convicted or even faced disciplinary action for their roles. In fact, the Porvenir Massacre represented how state authorities actively condoned such extrajudicial terror tactics against ethnic Mexicans out of hysteria over potential insurgent activity.

In more recent decades, with details and survivor testimonies finally being unearthed, a reckoning over the long-buried truth of Porvenir has slowly emerged. The Texas Rangers organization publicly acknowledged its role in 2018, a century after the massacre. While official historical markers were erected at the original village site memorializing the tragedy.

However, for many Mexican-American activists and descendants, these are seen as mere first steps in a long-overdue pursuit of justice, accountability and reconciliation over the bloodshed of Porvenir.

As new oral histories and official records continue being uncovered, the full scope of Porvenir's tragedy remains an open wound, a solemn reminder in this harsh desert landscape of what can happen when hatred lives unchecked and human life is rendered disposable.

A Day of Terror and Tragedy

One of the most violent and deadly days in Chicago's history unfolded a century ago along the segregated beaches and neighborhoods of the city's South Side on July 27th, 1919. What started as a confrontation over a young Black man swimming across an invisible racial divide quickly devolved into an outburst of racial violence, unrest and retaliation that left dozens dead and the city's tenuous race relations in ashes.

The inciting incident took place at the segregated 29th Street beach, where a group of Black teenagers defied racist social norms by crossing the invisible boundary separating the "white" and "colored" portions of the Lake Michigan shoreline waters. After rocks were thrown by white youth to drive them back, 17 year old Eugene Williams failed to heed their warnings and ended up struck and drowned.

What followed was a surge of escalating racial violence as outraged Black beachgoers were turned away by police while angry mobs of white youths roamed neighborhoods, pulling Blacks off streetcars, beating them and setting fires. As word of Williams' death spread, retaliatory attacks by Black residents commenced in kind.

By nightfall, Chicago had descended into all-out chaos, with rioters of both races rampaging in an orgy of arson, looting, gunfire and hand-to-hand brutality. Stores were ransacked, homes torched and innocents assaulted. The Illinois National Guard was eventually deployed onto the city's segregated South Side, but not before at least 38 were killed, 537 injured and millions in property damage inflicted over the course of nearly two weeks of anarchy.

While the eruption of racial hostilities in Chicago was shocking for its ferocity, the root causes were deeply systemic and long-simmering. The Great Migration of Southern Blacks northward had strained living conditions in already overcrowded and neglected Black neighborhoods while white residents harbored resentment over labor competition and threatened demographics. An atmosphere of economic insecurity combined with entrenched discriminatory policies and social codes set the combustible stage.

In the riots' aftermath, recriminations and efforts at reform fell drastically short of addressing the endemic issues. Over 500 were rendered homeless by arson, with public and private aid groups overwhelmed in providing relief. Legally, authorities succeeded in filing a mere 67 indictments in relation to the mass violence, with only a fraction convicted and recipients of lenient rulings.

Most damning was the refusal of city leaders and law enforcement to acknowledge systemic bias and racism as root factors enabling the events of that fateful July in 1919. While Chicago rebuilt, the scars of the race riots became embedded into the city's very fabric. More than 60,000 Black residents fled in the Great Migration's second wave in subsequent years. Both African American and white ethnics were left embittered for generations by the violence and lack of accountability.

Most tragically, the horrific events of July 27th served as a prologue for a century of segregation, housing discrimination and failed policies that have perpetuated cycles of crime, poverty and strained race relations on Chicago's South and West sides to the present day.

- Will Brown, victim of Omaha, Nebraska lynching

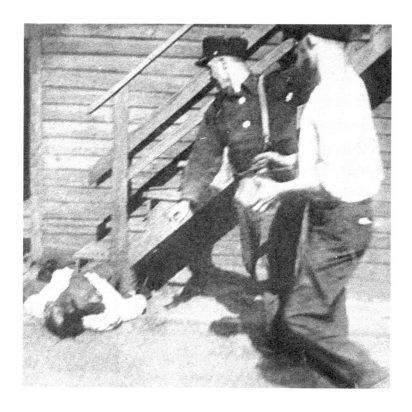

- African American being stoned by whites during 1919 Chicago race riot

Alwy M. Jones

Remembering the Elaine Massacre

Over a century ago, this small town in the fertile Arkansas Delta became the epicenter of one of the most violent and deadliest racial conflicts in American history. On September 30th 1919, a coordinated attack by white mobsters and state forces descended upon the Black sharecroppers of Elaine, intent on stamping out their fledgling labor organizing efforts through sheer brutality and terror.

What unfolded was a true massacre, upwards of 200 African American men, women and children slaughtered, hundreds more wounded, and a prosperous community razed over the span of several nights of unrelenting bloodshed. Corpses were left hanging from trees and railroad cars, victims shot at point-blank range, while Ku Klux Klan inspired mobs operated with impunity. The chain of events leading to the massacre traces back to the heavily oppressed Black sharecroppers in the Arkansas Delta. Exploited for their labor under a feudal-like system dominated by white landowners and merchants, whispers of unionizing to demand equitable payment circulated throughout the summer of 1919. Paranoia over a "Negro uprising" escalated after a tense confrontation between sharecroppers and landowners in a church.

On that fateful September evening in 1919, scores of white Missouri mobsters conspired with Arkansas' state militia and local vigilantes to execute a coordinated series of raids targeting any African Americans perceived as aligning with the sharecroppers' union. The so called "Elaine Riot" lasted for days, culminating in the brutal deaths of untold numbers of innocents, as well as thousands arrested and the complete dispossession and exile of the region's Black population.

In the aftermath, efforts at a federal investigation into the bloodbath were immediately suppressed. Up to 122 Black men were tried by an all-white state jury under farcical legal proceedings, with 12 sentenced to die by hanging for "insurrection" despite zero evidence they participated in any violence. Only the NAACP's relentless advocacy eventually saw the death sentences overturned in 1923 after three of the "Elaine 12" were executed.

This impunity and total lack of accountability for perpetrators represented how deeply systemic racism and violence toward African Americans remained entrenched across the reconstructed American South. Despite its scale and generational impacts, historians note how the Elaine Massacre was effectively whitewashed from the national consciousness, a mere footnote overshadowed by the Red Summer Riots occurring around the same period.

Today, beyond a modest memorial erected in recent decades, the physical reminders of the massacre that nearly depopulated Elaine's Black community have faded. But for descendent families scattered by the violence, the psychic scars remain raw when reflecting on their ancestors' untold hardship and the long, still unfinished march for true justice.

Alwy M. Jones

NEGROES PLAN TO KILL ALL WHITES

SLAUGHTER WAS TO BEGIN WITH 21 PROMINENT MEN AS THE FIRST VICTIMS.

"WE JUST BEGUN" PASSWORD

Blacks Had Armed Themselves and Planned to Kill Every White Person in Sight When Plot Was Exposed.

- Inflammatory newspaper headline in Elaine Race Riot of 1919. Headline and subtitles read: Negroes plan to kill all whites Slaughter was to begin with 21 prominent men as first victims. "We just begun" password Blacks Had Armed Themselves and Planned to Kill Every White Person in Sight When Plot Was Exposed.

Alwy M. Jones

Unearthing an American Racial Nightmare

For generations, a cloak of haunted silence has hung over this small town just outside Orlando. On the surface, Ocoee seems a sleepy, unassuming place but a century ago it bore witness to one of the most horrific and under reported episodes of racial violence in American history.

On November 2nd 1920, angered by a Black man's attempt to vote in the presidential election, a battalion of armed whites commenced a coordinated attack on Ocoee's prospering African American community, bound to violently preserve white supremacy at all costs. Over several nights of unchecked mob terror, families were massacred, homes and businesses burned to the ground. Hundreds were left homeless, their possessions looted and livelihoods erased in the bloody conflagration.

While the full death toll remains unconfirmed due to purposeful cover-ups, contemporary accounts suggest upwards of 60 Black residents were killed many at point-blank range while fleeing or surrendering. Entire blocks smoldered and bore the marks of immolation, with white vigilantes allowed free rein.

At the center of the brutality was the Sugar Mill ruins, the economic engine of Ocoee's once thriving Black community. Founded by affluent entrepreneur and descendent of slaves, Julius "July" Perry, the mill and surrounding district had grown into a proud emblem of Black independence and enfranchisement a reality intolerable to many of the area's most racist white residents.

Indeed, despite zero evidence Perry or residents had taken up arms, the mere presence of prosperous Black commerce and civic engagement was viewed as an existential threat to the region's entrenched system of white supremacy and Jim Crow subjugation. After Perry was savagely lynched on the eve of Nov 2nd, Ocoee's African American district saw no mercy in the coming nights' death march.

What's most unconscionable is how Florida state authorities and law enforcement actively participated or enabled the massacre, rather than preventing or stopping it. The few who faced legal repercussions amounted to a slap on the wrist. Official inquiries were immediately quashed by machinations of systemic racial injustice, with the bodies of victims left abandoned for vultures before makeshift grave sites were dug.

While the town of Ocoee indeed moved on, its hollowed ruins and secrets subsumed by fresh growth and development, the open wound left by the 1920 massacre has never truly healed. Streets and parks bear no memorial, acknowledgement or record of those killed. The true scope of the atrocity remains obscured behind a "respectable" front of manicured subdivisions.

Rosewood Massacre of 1923

In the early 20th century, racial tensions and segregation were rampant in the Deep South, including Florida. The African American town of Rosewood was a relatively safe haven, with Black families owning land, homes, and businesses. However, this prosperity was viewed as a threat by many whites in neighboring communities.

On January 1st 1923, a white woman in Sumner claimed that a Black man had assaulted her. Though she would later admit to fabricating the story, her initial claim ignited a powder keg of racial hatred. Bands of white men, many associated with the racist Ku Klux Klan, descended on Rosewood seeking revenge.

Armed whites from across the region poured into Rosewood, launching a horrific assault. They began burning homes and businesses, shooting residents on sight. Black families were dragged from their homes and executed. Those who fled were hunted through the woods like animals.

For seven nightmarish days, Rosewood was under siege by the racist mob. Homes and businesses were pillaged and burned to the ground. An unknown number of African Americans, some estimates as high as 150, were brutally murdered. Entire families were wiped out. The remaining residents were displaced, forced to flee for their lives.

In the wake of the violence, the town of Rosewood was a smoldering ruin. Very few structures remained standing. The lands and properties African American families had owned for generations were seized. Survivors were left homeless, traumatized, and destitute. No one from the mob ever faced legal consequences.

Catcher's Night of Racial Terror

In the early morning hours of December 29th, a mob of white men descended on the homes of African American families, unleashing a night of terror and bloodshed.

According to eyewitness accounts, the attack began around midnight, with the mob firing shots into residences and then dragging men, women and children from their homes. Over the next several hours, the mob beat, shot, mutilated and killed an untold number of Black citizens. Homes were set ablaze, personal property was destroyed, and survivors were left battered, bloody and homeless as the sun rose.

While a precise death toll remains unknown due to the chaos, it is clear this event represents one of the most horrific outbursts of racial violence in Arkansas history. Local sheriff's deputies allegedly took no action to intervene or protect the Black community that night.

Catcher's small African American community, which worked largely as sharecroppers on white owned cotton plantations, has been utterly devastated. Many survivors fled for their lives, leaving everything behind. Those who remained were traumatized, living in fear without shelter, food or medical care. Little was said officially by town leaders or state authorities in the wake of the tragedy. No arrests were made.

Civil rights activists strongly condemned the attack and accused local law enforcement of utterly failing to uphold the law and protect Black lives and property.

Despite some legal and political gains in the decades after the Civil War and abolition of slavery, the fundamental promise of equality and human rights for Black citizens remained unrealized. Racist ideologies of white supremacy still governed society, sanctioning the dehumanization, exploitation and ritual violence against people of color.

The Catcher massacre represents an especially egregious example of how the machinery of institutionalized racism continued to operate through intimidation, economic subjugation and physical terrorism toward any attempt by African Americans to assert their basic rights. The ability of white mobs to organize and act with total impunity is a chilling manifestation of the imbalance of power and lack of protection under the law for Black Americans.

Wounded Knee Massacre

What was meant as a peaceful transport of refugees to a new camp erupted into one of the most brutal massacres of Native Americans in United States history.

On the bitterly cold morning of December 29th, 1890, over 300 Lakota men, women and children were indiscriminately slaughtered by the U.S. 7th Cavalry Regiment. The death toll included at least 90 fatalities and many more wounded, making it one of the worst cases of institutionalized violence against First Nations peoples.

The massacre occurred as the 7th Cavalry attempted to disarm a band of around 350 Lakota Ghost Dancers, who were being relocated by force to a nearby military camp. The Ghost Dance was a widespread religious movement spreading across Native reservations, its members seeking to hasten the departure of Western settlers and a return to traditional ways of life.

According to eyewitnesses, a single shot was fired during the disarmament process. This single spark ignited a mass conflagration as the cavalry opened indiscriminate fire despite many of the Lakota already beginning to lay down their weapons.

The lopsided violence continued unabated for several hours until the Lakota's ammunition was depleted. Even then, the slaughter persisted in grotesque fashion as cavalrymen were ordered to pursue and execute remaining stragglers and wounded.

When the smoke finally cleared, Wounded Knee Creek essentially became one massive open grave site. The bodies of entire families, bands and tribes were left strewn across the lands they'd inhabited for centuries.

What's beyond dispute is the devastating loss of so many innocent lives cut down while peacefully practicing their beliefs including revered Chief Spotted Elk, who was among those massacred while taking no part in the disarmament.

Is this what America calls 'civilized'? To deal such cruelty upon those already confined, dislocated and stripped of their God given rights? The white man's brand of Christianity, rather than honoring the Prince of Peace, appears to only glorify massacre.

For many of the survivors and Lakota nation, this represented a harrowing culmination in the subjugation of their lands, spiritual traditions and way of life under the U.S. government's Indian Territory policies.

- Burial of the dead after the massacre of Wounded Knee. U.S. soldiers putting Indians in common grave; some corpses are frozen in different positions. South Dakota.

Alwy M. Jones

CIA's Hand in the Crack Epidemic

The 1980s crack cocaine crisis that ravaged America's inner cities and Black communities has long carried suspicions of a disturbing origin story. Now, decades later, mounting evidence suggests the U.S. government itself played a central, catalytic role in flooding African American neighborhoods with this potent, low-cost narcotic through unauthorized drug trafficking operations.

Investigations have uncovered how the Central Intelligence Agency's efforts to secretly arm and fund the Nicaraguan Contra rebels against the Sandinista government resulted in the proliferation of crack cocaine throughout cities like Los Angeles, Oakland, Detroit, Miami, and others with large Black populations. This flooding of the U.S. drug market with cheaply available cocaine represented one of the most destructive attacks on minority communities from within the government itself.

Beginning around 1984, a new and devastating form of cocaine rock or "crack" became widely available on the streets at low prices virtually overnight. The effects were rapidly apparent, as largely impoverished pockets of America's cities were besieged by individual addictions that quickly metastasized into epidemics of drug violence, gang warfare, decaying households, and widespread human misery.

According to a 1998 undercover probe by journalist Gary Webb, tons of cocaine were allowed to be smuggled into the U.S. by CIA operatives working with the Nicaraguan Contra rebels. The drugs were then distributed through LA street gangs like the Crips and Bloods to fund covert support for the rebels. An internal CIA report confirmed these ties to traffickers in 1987, but no substantial intervention took place until years later when crack was already a national crisis.

Federal reports have acknowledged that the Reagan administration's zeal for supporting the Contras helped birth the crack trade, regardless of the fallout on Black communities. The CIA's role from complicity to active participation remains fiercely debated and obfuscated by decades of cover-ups and Congressional stonewalling.

Beyond the immeasurable human toll of lives ruined, crack tore apart the economic and social fabric of countless urban communities. Crime rates soared as did rates of incarceration, broken families, impoverished households, and lost productivity. Some estimate the true societal costs reaching into the trillions.

The impact also set back budding efforts to reverse racist discrimination and empower Black economic mobility, as civil rights victories crumbled in a haze of addiction, hustling and carceral state marginalization. Hard fought gains were effectively reversed by powder that seeped like metaphoric kryptonite into disadvantaged communities.

While street level drug dealers and kingpins faced harsh criminal penalties, federal convictions for materially complicit government figures like Lt. Col. Oliver North in the Iran-Contra scandal were few and far between. No CIA personnel were ever charged for their involvement in turning a blind eye to cocaine trafficking used as a funding source.

This enduring sense of a two-tier justice system has only compounded Black mistrust in institutions many already viewed at best as apathetic to their needs, at worst actively discriminatory. Now decades later, drug policy experts see lingering cycles of deprivation, incarceration and despair as the bitter inheritance of those dark years.

As more information continues being uncovered through the declassification of records, one thread becomes undeniable, the same government sworn to protect America's cities instead enabled a narcotic pandemic that brought mass suffering upon the nation's already downtrodden. For the communities devastated by crack cocaine, the struggle for societal repair and generational healing is only just beginning.

Alwy M. Jones

Amritsar, India

In a brutal display of colonial force, British troops opened fire on a crowd of unarmed Indian civilians gathered at the Jallianwala Bagh gardens in Amritsar, massacring hundreds in an atrocity that will forever be seared into the conscience of the independence movement.

What began as a peaceful protest calling for democratic reforms and Hindu-Muslim unity rapidly descended into carnage as British Brigadier General Reginald Dyer ordered his troops to start firing without warning on the densely packed crowd hemmed into the urban park.

The troops first blocked the two exit points; men, women, children, everyone was falling around as the shooting went on relentlessly. It was true butchery in a space completely closed off, like helpless cattle.

Conservative estimates suggest at least 1,000 unarmed Indians were killed and over 1,200 more wounded, though the true death toll may never be known. The bullets even struck bystanders watching from neighboring homes and took the lives of babies and infants.

In the massacre's aftermath, Indians across the subcontinent reacted with mass protests, strikes and outrage over the British use of extreme force. The global shock and condemnation represented a pivotal moment that severely undermined British moral authority and control of the restive Indian populace.

While British civilian leaders like Winston Churchill initially condoned the massacre as necessary to maintain order over the "bankrupt" and "monstrous" independence movement, there was no denying the rising anti-colonial tide it produced across India.

Growing figures like Mohandas Gandhi and Jawaharlal Nehru led a surge in civil disobedience and demands for swaraj (self-rule) on the back of public fury over Amritsar. Annual protests and remembrances of the "Jallianwala Bagh Massacre Day" crystalized the move towards complete severance from the British Raj.

Though it took nearly 30 more years of struggle to drive out the Raj, historians widely agree the brutal Amritsar massacre was a pivotal turning point, awaking the Indian populace and forever destroying the moral justification for colonial occupation through its horrific violence and injustice.

As the dust settled on the bucolic grounds where over a thousand perished, Amritsar's scars would take decades to heal. But the massacre had only stoked the fires of Indian nationalism towards its inexorable march to independence from the British imperial yoke.

Appin, New South Wales

A dark cloud hangs over this remote frontier region in the wake of a brutal massacre that has potentially dire implications for relations between colonial settlers and the native Aboriginal populations of New South Wales.

In a series of raids and retaliatory attacks, groups of soldiers, settlers and former convicts systematically hunted down and slaughtered an estimated 25 Indigenous Dharawal people in the Appin area over several days and nights.

According to witnesses, the carnage began after colonial leaders received reports of attacks on settlers' huts and the killing of several settlers, supposedly by Dharawal warriors. In response, a heavily armed militia force was dispatched to the Dharawal lands to enact harsh reprisals.

It was nothing short of a full-scale massacre against our Indigenous people, the colonists showed no mercy, tracking down camp after camp and firing indiscriminately. Even women and young children were not spared from this unjust slaughter.

The exact sequence of events remains clouded as conflicting accounts emerged from both the Aboriginal survivors and the colonial militia involved. But it was clear the colonial forces overreacted with extreme deadly force that likely went far beyond the stated goal of apprehending a few Dharawal warriors accused of previous settler killings.

Local Dharawal elder Colebee, who had been working to maintain peace with the colonists, were captured and killed during the raids despite assisting the British. The white colonists claim they were enacting just punishments, but their actions show the unmistakable mark of race hatred fueling an indiscriminate slaughter of innocents.

Illawarra Region, New South Wales

The tranquil banks of the Minnamurra River were stained with innocent blood in another chapter of escalating frontier violence between British colonists and local Aboriginal tribes.

In a brutal act of retaliation, groups of settlers and former convicts massacred at least 14 Indigenous men, women and children from the area's Dharawal people in a series of raids and attacks over several days and nights.

Witnesses describe heavily armed militia parties sweeping through Dharawal camps and villages near the Minnamurra River, showing no mercy as they fired indiscriminately on families and used clubs and swords to butcher their victims. Their minds fevered with hate and hunger for their lands. Even the smallest infants were executed."

The massacre is said to have been sparked by the killing of several settlers in the area in the preceding weeks, which colonial authorities blamed on groups of Dharawal warriors enacting frontier resistance and reprisals.

However, local Aboriginal elders vehemently deny their people initiated any unprovoked violence, and say the settlers' scorched earth response was completely disproportionate and targeted innocents.

The colonial authorities, for their part, attempted to downplay and justify the killings, claiming they were merely keeping the peace by enacting "martial law" to punish Indigenous raiders threatening British sovereignty.

For the Indigenous survivors and their descendants in the Illawarra region, the appalling violence at Minnamurra River is seared into memory representing both a tragic loss and an inflection point that would further steal their multigenerational struggle to remain on and reclaim their sacred lands.

Tuskegee, Alabama

One of the most unethical and racially motivated medical research studies ever conducted on American soil; a 40-year government experiment that deliberately left hundreds of African American men with syphilis untreated in order to study the disease's impacts.

The details of what has become known as the "Tuskegee Study of Untreated Syphilis in the Negro Male" are as disturbing as they are difficult to fathom given modern ethical standards. Starting in 1932, the U.S. Public Health Service systematically recruited 600 impoverished Black sharecroppers from Macon County, Alabama, 399 with syphilis and 201 without the disease acting as a control group.

However, in a gross violation of research ethics, the men were actively deceived and denied access to readily available treatment and curative penicillin throughout the decade long study, even after the drug became the standard syphilis therapy by the 1940s. Their true ailments were disguised as "bad blood."

They were told they had a blood disorder and the government was looking to cure them, when all along they were just using them for laboratory rats to know how the disease works. According to reports, the PHS researchers' intended goal was to study the full pathology of untreated syphilis allowed to freely damage the human body over decades; all under the guise of providing the men with free meals, medical exams and burial payments as ethical enticements.

However, the means in which they carried out their observation were nightmarish by any humanitarian standard: Researchers actively prevented men from accessing syphilis treatment, switching them to ineffective remedies or even actively encouraging avoidance. When several men began receiving treatment from the draft office upon World War 2 conscription, researchers managed to have them stripped of their care.

The white doctors told them that getting penicillin from Uncle Sam might interfere with the studies, insisting that they should avoid it at all cost if they wanted their help. These were poor sharecropper with no means, they listened to their lies and paid the heaviest of prices.

Indeed, over the decades of secret observation, at least 28 directly died of syphilitic complications such as heart disease, blindness and insanity. Scores of wives and children also became infected after researchers actively withheld any warnings about contagiousness or provision of treatment.

When the study was finally exposed by whistleblowers in 1972, it ignited a firestorm of outrage that ricocheted across the African American community, the medical ethics establishment and through American race relations at large.

Coming on the heels of the civil rights movement era, the revelation of Tuskegee rocked the Black community's already tenuous trust in public health institutions and the U.S. government. For many, it seemed to confirm their worst suspicions about being actively persecuted by American biomedical authorities under the thin guise of science.

In 1973, the study was reluctantly terminated by an outcry of public revulsion and a major congressional hearing where the experiment's racist underpinnings and depraved ethics were laid bare for the world to witness.

A subsequent $10 million class-action settlement awarded to participants and their descendants did little to assuage the justified anger within African American communities. Widespread distrust of public health initiatives such as skepticism of urban vaccination programs became a predictable downstream effect plaguing policymakers for decades after.

The ramifications of U.S government making a mockery of human life and decency are still being felt today, both in generational trauma and a profound distrust of institutional medicine felt in too many communities of color, it reinforced the notion that the Black Community are seen as less than human, expendable guinea pigs in the eyes of the white establishment.

Alwy M. Jones

Church of England's Role in the Slave Trade

A dark chapter in the entwined histories of the Church of England and the British slave trade may finally be facing a reckoning after centuries of willful silence and moral contradiction.

New evidence and scholarly research is pulling back the veil on the Church's deep financial, logistical and even ideological entanglements supporting the horrors of Trans-Atlantic slavery throughout the 17th and 18th centuries. What's emerging is a damning portrait of religious complicity, profound hypocrisy and delayed justice.

For too long, the Church of England has been able to publicly maintain a posture of detached bystander to the abuses and human atrocities of Britain's slaving activity. However, the archival record makes abundantly clear its intimate economic and corporate ties underpinning this sinful capitalistic exploitation.

The Church as an institution developed profound financial interests in the success of the slave trade dating back to its very inception in the early 1600s. Individual bishops, clergy and parishes frequently invested in slaving companies like the Royal African Company, profiting handsomely from the enslaved labor that fueled the Caribbean plantation economies.

One of England's wealthiest endowments, the Church Commissioners fund, also held million-pound stakes in the South Sea Company, the British Empire's biggest slaving syndicate throughout the 18th century trafficking African captives to the Americas on its ships alone.

But the Church's relationship to slavery extended far beyond mere financial ties and material greed, many clergymen and laymen pushed pseudo-biblical rationalizations and racist dogma justifying the bondage of Africans as ethical and divinely ordained.

We find case after case of supposed men of God wielding scripture to subjugate fellow souls from Africa as fundamentally inferior and unequal beings, fit only for forced labor enriching their white Christian superiors.

Foremost among those voices stood Bishop of Exeter John Thomas, whose widely distributed 1792 pamphlet "On the Scriptural Justification For Most Lawful Trade in Negro Slaves and Perpetual Servitude" weaved racist dogma and bastardized biblical passages to endorse the entire ecosystem of kidnapping, branding, chaining and brutalizing millions of Africans. Thomas and voices like his in Church ranks dismissed the humanity of African people, painting their captors as anointed avatars of Christ spreading civilization. They endorsed grotesqueries like violent coercion over conversion, wanton family separations, and the systematic rape and breeding of enslaved women.

Even after the 1807 Act abolished the slave trade and 1833 Slavery Abolition Act outlawed possession of human property across the Empire, too many Church officials and laymen still clung to racism, justifying segregation and imperialist oppression of Afro-Caribbean people through theological double-talk.

According to critics, it took the Church of England over two centuries to even begin atoning on an institutional level by apologizing for its wealth founded on enslaved labor and offering reparations. Many say much more truth and reconciliation efforts are still required.

With more and more evidence emerging about the Church's varied degrees of complicity and financial entwinement with slavery's evils, many see the scales beginning to lift from willfully blind eyes towards an unavoidable historical reckoning.

Alwy M. Jones

Boer War Tactics Foreshadowed 20th Century's Darkest Atrocities

The Second Boer War remains a conflict whose bitter legacy continues drawing scrutiny from historians. Chief among the controversies was the scorched-earth strategy employed by British forces under the leadership of General Lord Horatio Kitchener; including the creation of what were then called "concentration camps" that foreshadowed some of the 20th century's worst humanitarian atrocities.

Kitchener oversaw the mass internment of tens of thousands of Boer civilians; primarily women and children into a network of overcrowded, poorly supplied camps across South Africa. Combined with the devastating combat losses inflicted by superior British firepower, these harsh tactics contributed to the deaths of over 26,000 Boer republican men, women and children by the war's conclusion.

It represented the British empire at its most brutally racist and uncompromising. For Kitchener and his high command, it mattered little how many civilian lives were sacrificed to break the Boers' resistance and shore up imperial dominance.

Amid the escalating guerilla campaign waged by Boer fighters after the British captured key cities like Johannesburg and Pretoria, Kitchener's strategy centered on depriving the highly mobile Boers of food, supplies and civilian cover by systematically burning Boer farms and interning their populations.

Over 60 tented camps were rapidly erected across South Africa to house these displaced persons.

Lack of planning and severe overcrowding, with tens of thousands crammed into squalid conditions, caused outbreaks of disease like typhoid, cholera and dysentery to rage unchecked. Food and medical provisions were chronically inadequate. Photographs from the time show emaciated children dying by the scores.

While concentration camps as detainment facilities for civilian populations had existed previously, the Second Boer War marked the first time this tactic had been institutionalized across an entire nation. Some historians contend Kitchener's policies amounted to ethnic cleansing, if not outright genocide targeting Boer identity itself.

Humanitarian campaigners like Emily Hobhouse wrote scathing reports likening the conditions inside to extermination camps. This international condemnation, coupled with Westminster politics, eventually pressured the government to improve camp conditions and ultimately pursue a negotiated peace.

Still, the episode remains a dark stain on British imperial history, and an ominous early preview of the 20th century's worst atrocities and crimes against humanity yet to come. Experts note chilling similarities between the arbitrary internment and mass civilian deaths in South Africa's camps with the genocidal horrors that unfolded under the Nazis, Pol

Pot's Khmer Rouge regime, and other modern genocides.

Tragically, these tactics arose not from revolutionary hatreds, but from the well-established racism and dehumanization that colonizers inflicted upon colonized peoples. British field marshals like Kitchener likely had little notion of the 20th century's genocidal horrors they were in a sense prefiguring."

For South Africa itself, the concentration camps remain not just symbolic of the oppression and brutality of British rule, but the nation's own foundation upon which the structures of institutionalized racism were built. The Boer republics' surrender ceded territories and mineral rights to the British, enabling discriminatory policies that flowed into apartheid's creation.

This complex legacy has fueled both commemoration and controversy in contemporary South Africa. While some Boer descendants annually memorialize ancestors killed in the camps as patriotic victims, the African National Congress has criticized these events for overlooking how white oppression was eventually codified through apartheid's formation.

At the sites of former concentration camps like Bethulie, memorials have been established. But they are also somber reminders of colonialism's darkest excesses, a preview of the industrialized genocides and cruelties yet to come in the age of global warfare and nationalist hatred.

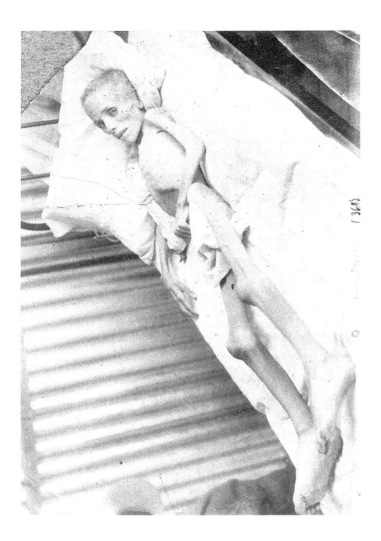

- Lizzie van Zyl, visited by Emily Hobhouse in a British concentration camp.

Alwy M. Jones

Economic Strangulation Shattered Morale, Fueled Extremism

The "Hunger Blockade" imposed by British naval forces during the First World War remains one of the most controversial and haunting chapters of modern European history. By strangling Germany's access to vital imported foodstuffs and raw materials over four years, this maritime siege inflicted immense suffering and deprivation upon the German civilian population. Its effects would reshape the nation's economy, political landscape and psyche in ways still felt a century later.

When the blockade was launched by the British shortly after war broke out in 1914, its stated goal was to weaken Germany economically and break the will of its populace to continue the military conflict. What ensued was a gradual descent into mass hunger, malnutrition and collateral devastation impacting all segments of civilian society.

As German ports were cut off from international trade, shortages of essentials like grains, meat, fats, fertilizers, and fuel compounded rapidly. Bread rations steadily shrunk while prices for black market foodstuffs became outrageously inflated. Ersatz imitation products made from inadequate ingredients became dietary staples.

Historical records indicate average caloric intake plummeted below sustenance levels. Epidemics of tuberculosis and influenza ravaged populations weakened by malnutrition. Food riots became commonplace as did desperate measures like stripping public parks of their fauna to find nourishment.

Official statistics show upwards of 750,000 German civilians may have perished from causes directly tied to the Allied naval blockade and associated deprivations. Yet some historians argue these figures drastically underestimate the true death toll from malnutrition-induced diseases and respiratory illnesses like the 1918 flu pandemic.

Beyond direct health impacts, the blockade's economic toll proved catastrophic. Industrial productivity faltered as workers grew too malnourished and sick. Agricultural output nosedived from lack of fertilizer and draft animals. Trade virtually ceased beyond the most critical war materials.

For the German public, the feeling of being besieged and abandoned by the outside world fostered intense bitterness and resentments. Morale deteriorated alongside the material deprivations gripping the home front. Severe psychological damage manifested in trauma, political extremism and a profound loss of faith in institutions.

Given the blockade's pivotal role in ultimately forcing Germany's military capitulation, the dire conditions it created have been viewed by some as an excessive humanitarian catastrophe upon civilians. However, others maintain the hunger blockade remained a justifiable wartime measure of economic warfare to defeat an opponent perpetrating its own atrocities.

Nevertheless, its destructive social and economic legacy persisted long after the armistice. The blockade helped fuel the rise of radical ideologies like Nazism, who channeled lingering resentment over Germany's treatment by the Allies into a thirst for retaliation and reverence. Its traumatic impacts propagated cycles of destitution, national humiliation and political extremism.

Alwy M. Jones

Hague Rules Blurred as Civilians Paid Tragic Price

The shadows of history still linger in this iconic city's skeletal ruins and stone scars. The Bombing of Dresden in 1945 represented one of the most controversial and ethically fraught episodes of aerial warfare in World War II. In the waning months of the conflict in Europe, hundreds of RAF and U.S. Army Air Force bombers unleashed a torrent of incendiary bombs and high explosives on the urban center reducing vast portions to smoldering rubble while inflicting staggering civilian casualties.

Though the intended targets included factories, railways and military infrastructure, the saturation bombardment over two days created apocalyptic firestorms that devoured neighborhoods, churches, hospitals and cultural monuments. Conservative estimates indicate over 25,000 residents perished in the infernos, with other figures suggesting the death toll exceeded 100,000.

For decades, debate has raged over whether the Allies violated internationally recognized rules of engagement and military necessity by devastating a city of relatively minor strategic importance at such a late stage of the war. Dresden's symbolic tragedy has become inextricably intertwined with the ethics and laws surrounding the targeting of civilians; issues still highly relevant in modern conflicts.

The bombing exemplified a dark new calculus emerging from the cauldron of total war. Military forces no longer simply defeated an enemy's armies, but professed the need to break the spine of their society as a whole even at the cost of once sacrosanct humanitarian rules.

Prior to World War I, the international community championed strict codes established by the 1899 and 1907 Hague Conventions designed to protect civilian populations during warfare. These prohibited the "attack or bombardment of towns, villages, dwellings or buildings which are undefended," except when locations possessed significant military value.

However, the industrialized carnage of WWI eroded these codes. Both sides routinely shelled towns, massacred civilians, and expanded the theater of combat to homes and workplaces. The 1945 bombing of Dresden continued this escalating pattern where the entire urban environment was targeted and viewed as part of an enemy's economic "fortification" even as Nazi Germany neared final collapse.

In the bombing's aftermath, Nazi propaganda seized upon the civilian toll to denounce Allied "terror bombing" while downplaying German atrocities. Later theories suggested Dresden was targeted as retribution for bombing campaigns Germany inflicted earlier in the war.

Yet the majority view among Allied high commands at the time appeared to rationalize the city's destruction as a means to leverage maximum economic damage and degrade enemy morale. Military leaders like British Air Marshall Sir Arthur "Bomber" Harris viewed any urban area as a legitimate and deserving target due to potential contributions to Germany's war industry.

"The days of keeping war confined to the battlefield are over," Harris notoriously declared in support of area bombardment tactics. "The great German cities have been turned into defensive frontlines and must be erased."

Still, the bombing campaigns of WWII clearly reopened long-standing ethical fissures around the just applications of modern military force. The victors may dictate histories, but images of Dresden's sepulcher-like ruins permanently scarred the global conscience, fueling important re-examinations and re-interpretations of the laws of warfare.

In the decades since, the international community has sought to further codify protections for noncombatants. This included the 1949 Geneva Conventions establishing humanitarian safeguards, and subsequent statutes like the 1977 Additional Protocols governing the principles of distinction and proportionality during military operations.

Alwy M. Jones

1948 Killings of Civilians Revealed Darker Side of Colonial Policing

In this rural village northwest of Kuala Lumpur, annual ceremonies are still held honoring the unarmed villagers who perished in a massacre carried out by a British military patrol over seven decades ago. The tragic events of December 11th 1948 have become permanently seared into the national consciousness of modern Malaysia, representing one of the British Empire's most notorious acts of violence against civilians during its waning colonial era.

What began as a routine Operation by British Commonwealth troops to locate communist insurgents during the ongoing Malayan Emergency soon descended into inexplicable brutality. After surrounding the rubber plantation village of Batang Kali and detaining its residents for screening, evidence suggests the Scots Guards unit summarily executed numerous men over the course of several hours' execution style.

Among the victims were elderly civilians like 73 year old Siah Khamis, as well as a Chinese family of four. The reasons cited in official reports remain dubious at best, ranging from outright fabrications to paranoia over one of the detainees attempting escape. No evidence ever materialized that any villagers were involved in armed resistance against British rule.

In the ensuing decades, the Batang Kali massacre was swept under the rug of colonial secrecy and misinformation by British authorities with an initial cover-up portraying the victims as communist insurgents killed in a shootout. Only through the intrepid investigations of journalists, human rights advocates and Malaysian officials did a full public accounting gradually emerge.

However, it wasn't until 1970 that British authorities acknowledged any wrongdoing following an official government inquiry. And still today, the United Kingdom has never formally apologized to the victims' families nor accounted for the chain of command specifically authorizing such unjustifiable lethal force. When sovereign powers perceive themselves as dealing with lesser human beings, moral compasses can become dangerously deregulated. The Batang Kali massacre was a grave milestone documenting how civilian lives were utterly devalued under the colonial chauvinism mindset.

Beyond its individual cruelty, the massacre carried generational impacts reverberating across Malaya's eventual path to independence in 1957. It exacerbated grievances among the ethnic Chinese and Malay populations chafing under heavy-handed British suppression tactics during the 12 year Emergency conflict with communist militants. While Commonwealth troops ultimately prevailed in defeating the insurgency, the violence and rights abuses were sowing fertile ground for rising nationalist liberation sentiments. Batang Kali became a rallying symbol generating support for self-governance free from such draconian foreign occupation.

In post-colonial Malaysia, the massacre has endured as a national tragedy enshrined in school textbooks and cultural memory. The Commonwealth War Graves Commission still maintains the memorial plot where victims were hastily buried, acknowledging the massacre as "one of the darkest episodes" during British rule in the region. Yet successive British governments have refused calls by Malaysian officials and human rights groups to officially apologize or pay compensation to survivors and relatives of the dead. In 2014, lawsuits seeking accountability from London were dismissed on technical grounds without the case hearing evidence; drawing renewed condemnations. With its graphic violence and apparent senselessness, the Batang Kali massacre indeed stands as a sobering study in how even modern nation states can suspend civilized norms when maintaining power over subject peoples. Its wounds remain unhealed largely because truths and full accountability remained obstructed by systemic indifference.

As one of the final spasms of Britain's colonial legacy, Batang Kali delivered an indelible human reminder; that the veneer of imperial benevolence could abruptly shatter into utter depravity. Malaysia remains a living case study analyzing how such historical wrongs at once unite and divide a multifaceted society.

- Royal Marine poses holding severed heads during the Malayan Emergency

Alwy M. Jones

Mau Mau Repression Bred Cycles of Trauma

For decades, the full barbarity of British detention tactics used to crush the Mau Mau anti-colonial uprising in 1950s Kenya remained an officially sanctioned secret. Only years after the East African nation achieved independence has the veil been lifted fully on the widespread use of systematic torture, violence and dehumanization by colonial authorities against civilians; both rebel fighters and non-combatants alike.

What has emerged is one of the darkest, most unapologetically brutal chapters in the British Empire's final violent gasps to retain autocratic control over its overseas territories. Operating under broad "emergency" powers, British soldiers, police and administrators waged a scorched-earth campaign to extinguish the Mau Mau rebellion and its demands for Kenyan self-rule and land reform.

From 1952-1960, this counterinsurgency operation included mass detention of over 100,000 people in appalling camp complexes across the Kenyan countryside. Remote facilities became horrific epicenters designed for both isolating insurgents and quite literally beating the defiance out of the local population through unconscionable methods.

Their daily existence involved being caged in tiny sheds, enduring constant physical abuse, malnourishment and untreated diseases, they were not considered human beings with dignity, but animals fit for only obedience.

Survivors and historical evidence confirm that detainees; many imprisoned on flimsy pretexts, routinely faced extreme corporal punishments for perceived insolence or withholding information. Common torture techniques included stress positions, beatings with clubs, whipping, mauling by dogs, starvation, castration threats, and sexual assault. Thousands of deaths due to systemic abuses like these were covered up over the years.

While Britain sought militarily to wipe out the Mau Mau insurgency and its adherents, many experts contend the heavier objective involved crushing a broader psychological resistance to continued colonial subjugation. Humiliation and torture were seemingly employed as deliberate counter-incentives to nationalist Kenyans' demands for self-determination and land redistribution.

The detention camps were very much about dehumanizing native populations so they could be effectively re-indoctrinated into accepting their eternal exploitation as subjects of empire, while prisons existed to punish, these camp hellholes were designed to obliterate any inkling of human dignity.

The British government long dismissed these torture accusations as unsubstantiated propaganda or "exaggerations." Only recently has evidence like archival documentation forced British authorities to admit instructing systemic use of such grotesque tactics under the guise of colonial security enforcement.

In 2013, the British government formally apologized and paid reparations to over 5,200 elderly Kenyans who were brutalized under colonial detention, the first time it granted legal reparations to colonial-era torture survivors. Many more victims passed beyond the window of eligibility, their opportunities for closure or justice permanently sealed.

Each criminal act of barbarism acknowledged unveils just the tip of the mountain of depraved and dehumanizing tactics the empire felt entitled to inflict on its colonial subjects. The long-term emotional crucifixions surely multiplied the physical death tolls across multiple generations.

Indeed, the decades long government cover up compounded the anguish for victims' families deprived of validating and memorializing their loved ones' ordeals. Now exposed abuses have re-opened floodgates of intergenerational trauma, hardened political divisions and a fundamental distrust of state authority among the Kikuyu ethnic group targeted in the Mau Mau crackdown.

For modern Kenya, the reckoning has sparked fraught but necessary reckonings on how to heal these persistent wounds and honestly confront its violent path from colony to independent nation.

Demands for meaningful truth and reconciliation processes have come from various quarters, including granting more reparations, erecting memorials, instituting school curricula on British atrocities, and pursuing further archaeological investigations into clandestine detention sites to identify the unreported dead.

As Britain itself continues reckoning with its colonial legacies, the Mau Mau uprising and its vicious suppression will forever stand as an indelible blot on its moral authority, particularly in the arena of human rights and just governance of democratic institutions. The cycles of violence begun in detention camps which became harbingers of woes later visited upon British society itself through racial unrest and political extremism.

Alwy M. Jones

U.S. Military Sexual Assaults Leave Lasting Scars in Okinawa

On an island hosting one of the United States' largest and most strategically significant military presences abroad, a dark undercurrent afflicts the relationship between American forces and the local population. Incidents of sexual violence perpetrated by U.S. troops against Okinawan civilians, particularly women and young girls, have represented a longstanding source of outrage, resentment and soul-searching about the human costs of this overseas installation.

The tiny island region has hosted a substantial U.S. military presence since the brutal Battle of Okinawa ended World War II in 1945 after a horrific civilian death toll. Over 50,000 American troops are currently based at facilities making up 20% of Okinawa's land mass, despite local advocacy aimed at reducing this footprint.

But it has been a pattern of sexual assaults and related criminal behavior by U.S. personnel that has spawned the most vitriol. According to Pentagon data, nearly 600 service members or contractors based in Okinawa have faced charges for sex crimes over the past 50 years, including rapes, sexual assaults and exploitation of minors.

The crimes span horrific cases like the 2008 gang rape of a 14-year old girl by four U.S. sailors, the 2005 indecent assault of a Filipino barmaid, and the infamous 1995 abduction and rape of a 12-year-old

Okinawan schoolgirl by three servicemen. The perpetrators received varied sentences, but the psychological scars inflicted by each incident compounded an overarching sense of violation.

Periodic uproars over these incidents have erupted for decades, generating massive protests and calls for reducing or outright removing American military influence from Okinawa. While the U.S. has taken some accountability steps including improved prevention training and security reforms, each new crime has fueled mistrust and doubts over their seriousness.

Indeed, some historians and political theorists have drawn parallels between the issue of U.S. military sexual violence and the attitudes that previously enabled systemic exploitation of native populations under traditional imperial constructs. Where local women and children were treated as objects to service a transient force of mostly male soldiers.

To some extent the crisis reflects the same tensions that often accompany interactions between troops and civilians amid any martial environment. Incidents of sexual misconduct have long plagued militaries including the American armed forces internally. Stringent prevention and accountability policies have struggled to fundamentally reshape institutional cultures permissive of such crimes.

However, observers contend the presence of foreign troops with limited local ties and accountability exacerbates these problems exponentially.

Disagreements over prosecutorial jurisdiction have created legal gray areas where justice is delayed or denied. Socioeconomic and racial divides segregate Okinawan and U.S. military communities, fueling misunderstandings and mistrust on both sides.

As Okinawa continues grappling with the ripple effects of serial sexual violence, paths forward remain fraught. There are calls for greater civilian oversight and adjudication over military courts, transitioning bases' functional roles toward more economic development, renegotiating the terms of American presence overall.

But for many Okinawans, the traumas inflicted represent a deeper loss of their homeland's autonomy and self-determination. The legacy of wartime oppression has persisted into cycles of resentment destined to continue for as long as outside forces violate their human sanctity.

Alwy M. Jones

Rape Allegations against UK Troops in Kenya Ignite Calls for Justice

In the shadow of Mount Kenya, where the British military has maintained a presence for over half a century, searing accusations of sexual violence against local women have shattered the naïve assumptions surrounding these enduring training operations. Over the past recent years, reports have steadily emerged of Kenyan civilians including underage victims; who say they were sexually assaulted, exploited or even raped by visiting UK troops.

Such allegations carry traumatic human costs in their own right. But the alleged perpetrators' ties to a foreign military force largely unbound by local jurisdiction has ignited wider scrutiny over imbalanced power dynamics and systemic injustices rooted in the same colonial legacies that first established these rural garrison towns as epicenters serving the Crown's training demands.

To date, over 600 individual abuse allegations encompassing a range of sexual offenses have been levied against British army instructors and infantry battalions rotating through Nanyuki and other long-standing military installations in Kenya's former Central Province and Rift Valley regions.

Many of the most disturbing cases involve adult soldiers accused of raping underage girls from nearby villages. An Associated Press investigation documented exploitation of girls as young as 12 traded for things as petty as bakery goods or tomatoes in squalid shantytowns located just outside British base perimeters.

The men wave some coins or sweets before these children coming from utter poverty, acting as if that absolves the criminality of their actions. The damage inflicted on young souls already conditioned to powerlessness simply doesn't register on their human conscience. Other accusations range from rapes of Kenyan service staffers working on bases, to mysterious pregnancies of local teens solicited by soldiers from notorious local clubs and brothels frequented by troops on leave.

While UK military officials have pledged to fully investigate all credible allegations, thus far relatively few charges appear substantiated beyond a smattering of court Martials and dishonorable discharges. Much of the foot-dragging on accountability stems from entrenched barriers to reporting and pursuing legal redress when crimes are committed.

Due to a controversial longstanding agreement ceding local jurisdiction to the UK judicial system, Kenyan authorities remain largely powerless to prosecute offending soldiers directly. The Visiting Forces Act established during British colonial rule exempts troops from Kenyan civilian laws and law enforcement except for serious crimes like murder.

This dynamic has nurtured an impunity enabling abuses to persist through systematic obfuscation according to rights advocates. They point to how victims seeking legal recourse are often rebuffed, ignored or subjected to implicit biases and "virginity testing" from investigators. The rule of law surrounding off-base misconduct appears designed primarily to insulate British forces rather than deliver meaningful justice.

Such attitudes parallel broader societal beliefs around male sexuality and power that enable rape cultures. But some analysts contend the roots of this dynamic in Kenya run deeper still into its colonial past when indigenous women and girls were tacitly seen as existing to fulfill auxiliary "comfort" roles for white colonial officers.

The irony remains that the British military maintains these Kenyan facilities ostensibly to assist in training missions combatting global security threats and upholding democratic principles. However, its record on basic accountability and human rights in these very host communities reveals a dissonance exacerbating instability.

When foreign deployments charged with exporting rule of law actively erode standards through sexual violence, it corrodes the moral authorities and state-building objectives they claim to represent. Such abuses render credibility and alliances expendable in the pursuit of credible peace, justice and human security for all populations.

As shocking testimony continues emerging from Kenya's rural military landscapes, the British government now faces withering international condemnation over its initial stonewalling of these endemic allegations. UK military officials have been accused of burying evidence to conceal the full scope and seemingly lax standards.

Under mounting pressure, Britain eventually initiated an independent probe overseen by a retired judge. But many Kenyans remain skeptical that true deterrence and accountability can be achieved under a prosecution system steeped in the legacies of the very power structures enabling the original exploitation.

Alwy M. Jones

Abu Ghraib Torture Stigma Persists as Rallying Cry against Injustice

The indelible images retain their power to shock the conscience nearly two decades later; bloodied and humiliated Iraqi detainees, subjected to grotesque human indignities and tortures at the hands of U.S. military personnel tasked with upholding democratic values and the rule of law. The 2003 Abu Ghraib prison scandal ignited global outrage not just over the graphic abuses themselves, but what they symbolized about America's flailing moral standing and accountability in its tragically misguided occupation of Iraq.

Human rights activists argue the United States has yet to fully reckon with or absorb the scandal's searing lessons on the systemic perils of unchecked power detached from impartial oversight. While several lower ranking soldiers ultimately faced legal consequences, the institutional failures enabling Abu Ghraib's horrors from muddied interrogation standards to leadership breakdowns were never comprehensively addressed according to experts.

Abu Ghraib exposed the malignancy when detached forces pursue security objectives through any means they determine as expedient, regardless of obligations under international law. State sanctioned torture not only degrades individuals, it compromises the entire moral credibility of state powers.

Alwy M. Jones

The first cryptic photos depicting U.S. soldiers' dehumanizing treatment of Iraqi detainees outside Baghdad emerged in early 2004, shared via anonymous upload to online websites and news outlets. But it wasn't until 60 Minutes II aired Joseph Darby's shocking firsthand digital images in April of that year that the world's attention finally galvanized around the apparent war crimes unfolding at Abu Ghraib.

Images like "The Man on the Box," showing prisoners contorted into dehumanizing "stress positions," quickly became iconic symbols of what President George W. Bush administration officials dismissively labeled as mere "disgraceful" instances of unsanctioned abuse.

But subsequent investigations by the U.S. military as well as media reports and human rights organizations like Amnesty International and Human Rights Watch ultimately uncovered a systematic pattern of abuses that extended well beyond the actions of low ranking "bad apples." Evidence pointed to confusing rules of engagement that dangerously blurred lines around acceptable interrogation techniques and essentially incentivized prisoner mistreatment.

From forced sexual humiliation to severe beatings, psychological torment, even homicides, Abu Ghraib revealed a profoundly dehumanizing environment where U.S. forces devalued Iraqi lives to simply mean toward ill-defined ends. These weren't isolated actions but ones cultivated and emboldened by leadership failures on every level that remain unresolved today.

Court martials and prosecutions resulted in convictions for 11 U.S. Army personnel, including iconic villains like Lynndie England; infamously photographed leading a naked Iraqi prisoner around on a leash. But no higher-ranking officers or civilian leaders were held accountable. Even today, key Bush administration figures like Secretary of Defense Donald Rumsfeld maintain they bore no direct responsibility for policies many consider unlawful.

The abuses at Abu Ghraib also underscored the vulnerabilities of civilian detainees in armed conflicts whose status falls into legal gray areas not fully protected by the Geneva Conventions at the time. Critics argue insufficient safeguards and enforceable deterrents enabled U.S. personnel to depict Iraqi prisoners as sub-human "unlawful combatants."

Allowing moral relativism to infiltrate military cultures creates slippery slopes where indignities quickly escalate from benign forms of torture to sadism justifying killing of detainees are no longer useful. It demonstrates the universal need to strengthen international legal frameworks for protecting all civilians against depravities of conflict zones."

Yet troubling replicates of institutional breakdowns enabling abuses have since materialized in other theaters, including CIA "black sites", Guantanamo Bay, and even domestic immigrant detention facilities. For many, it confirms a failure of the international justice system to evolve credible, binding enforcement mechanisms capable of deterring human rights violations by rogue actors.

Abuse scandals persist because the structures permitting them remain deeply embedded across security state apparatuses and their unchecked exceptionalism. Whether it's Abu Ghraib, CIA torture, Guantanamo or extraordinary rendition; injustices proliferate if accountability remains aspirational rather than binding.

Back in Iraq, the legacy of Abu Ghraib's torture has calcified into yet another open wound for the country's civic spirit and cultural psyche. On the 2009 anniversary, former detainees and Iraqi political figures gathered to dedicate a permanent memorial depicting the iconic torture images along with translations into Arabic and poetry dedicated to the victims.

Many view the memorial located on the grounds where the notorious prison once stood after its demolition as not just bearing witness to an American military lapse, but a universal symbol against state perpetuated injustice that transcends any conflict.

The solidarity of shared human suffering is eternal, as are the lessons we must keep instilling on the need to constrain unchecked power through the force of moral justice. Only then can the souls subjected to Abu Ghraib's depravity finally find the peace and dignity denied to them in life.

Alwy M. Jones

Bosnia's Genocide Scars Remain Unhealed Decades Later

In this small town situated within the Drina Valley, the specter of unimaginable atrocities hovers as inescapably as the morning fog. Srebrenica was the epicenter of genocidal ethnic cleansing and mass killings that revealed the depths of inhumanity lying just beneath the surface of Yugoslavia's implosion.

In July 1995, a brutal campaign by the Bosnian Serb Army culminated in the calculated massacre of over 8,000 Bosnian Muslim civilians seeking refuge under the protection of a designated UN "safe area." The slaughter committed over a mere few days represented both the worst act of genocide against civilians since World War II and the most brazen defiance of international humanitarian laws in modern times.

But let it happen the world did, as lightly armed Dutch peacekeepers proved no match against Bosnian Serb forces led by General Ratko Mladic. Mladic embraced his self-styled persona as the "Butcher of Bosnia," orchestrating meticulously planned mass shootings, torture and wholesale expulsions of Muslims. Tens of thousands were forcibly displaced from homes and ancestral villages.

The savagery sparked instinctive human outcry, yet this alone proved inadequate to halt the mechanized slaughter. Mladic operated under the unabashed protection of former Serbian strongman Slobodan

Milosevic, whose "Greater Serbia" aspirations emboldened such eliminationism methods for homogenizing territories through terror.

In Srebrenica alone, recently uncovered and re-exhumed mass graves point to over 40 distinct execution sites where Muslims were summarily bound, beaten and dispatched at point-blank range by Serb forces. Many were instructed to remove personal effects, reassured they were simply being "transferred." Documented instances of rape and child murders were not uncommon.

Though the genocide represented an undeniable nadir precipitating greater international intervention, the conflict's embers continued smoldering through fractured cease-fires and uneasy NATO peacekeeping deployments for years to come. It would take until 2001 for Milosevic to be apprehended and face genocide charges before the Hague Tribunal; charges for which he never lived to be convicted.

And while General Mladic was eventually arrested over a decade later by Serbian security forces and ultimately convicted on charges of genocide and crimes against humanity, many see his combined 40 year prison sentence as meager restitution. His defenders remain ardently unrepentant even today.

Alwy M. Jones

The Dark Legacy of the Chetnik Movement During World War II in Yugoslavia.

The Chetniks began as a royalist and Serbian nationalist resistance group led by Dragoljub "Draza" Mihailovic following the Axis invasion of Yugoslavia in 1941. While initially allied with the communist-led Partisans against the occupiers, the Chetniks soon turned their aim toward securing an ethnically homogeneous Greater Serbia.

As the war raged on, the Chetniks became increasingly collaborationist with the Italian and German forces in a brutal campaign of ethnic cleansing targeting non-Serbs, particularly Bosnians, Croats and Albanians. A number of Jews served among the Chetnik ranks. Their atrocities were widespread and savage.

In August 1941, Chetnik forces carried out a massacre of over 500 civilians, including children, in Susnjar and neighboring villages in Herzegovina. Eyewitness accounts describe victims being burned alive and mutilated.

The Chetnik "Case White" operation from January to February 1943 saw the forced expulsion and murder of thousands of non-Serb civilians in eastern Bosnia. Entire villages were razed.

Perhaps their most infamous act was the Chetnik massacre of up to 68,000 Muslim civilians in the

Bihac region of Bosnia in 1941-1942 under Chetnik General Vasilije Vesovic.

These are just a few of the many documented large-scale atrocities and ethnic cleansing campaigns carried out by the Chetniks during the war under the pretext of an ethnically pure Greater Serbia.

In the aftermath, the devastation and displacement of entire communities left a lasting legacy of trauma, resentment and sectarian strife that still reverberates today in the Balkans. The Chetnik period was one of the darkest chapters of World War II.

- Chetniks in Sumadija kill a Partisan through heart extraction.

- Another Chetnik group killing an unarmed civilian.

Alwy M. Jones

Agent Orange and the Poisoning of Vietnam

What falls from the sky as a mist can prove far more deadly than any bomb. In the jungles of Vietnam, a chemical tactic that turned foliage into the enemy and the costs that contaminated the land for generations.

Day after day, low-flying crop dusters unleashed a downpour of herbicides, codenamed the ominously colorful "Agent Orange." The goal was to defoliate the dense jungle canopy and expose any Viet Cong guerillas lurking below. But this supposed "force augmentation" yield devastating and indiscriminate collateral damage.

In villages like Trang Bang, the spraying decimated crops and killed livestock, leaving innocent families suddenly starving. Even more horrifically, the dioxin-laced chemicals caused gruesome injuries and birth defects among civilians exposed to the toxins.

Years later, as Frey's healthy daughter was born with deformed reproductive organs, he felt his military service extract a permanent cost. "It felt like a cruel injustice to our own family," he said, voice shaking. "How many victims are still unknown?"

Such stories across Vietnam, where over 20% of jungles and 10% of villages were exposed to Agent Orange with massively elevated rates of cancer, nerve disorders, and generational birth defects. Yet the U.S. manufacturers have dodged accountability, reaching a settlement but admitting no wrongdoing.

Maj. Gen. John D. Murray, once a key planner for Operation Ranch Hand, has since lamented using these "inhumane damn chemicals" that have devastated both friendly and enemy lives.

Alwy M. Jones

Legal Battle over Drowned Captives Exposed System's Moral Depravity

In late 1781, as the British slave ship Zong entered Caribbean waters after departing from modern-day Ghana, her crew faced a hellish decision borne from the unfathomable inhumanity of the Trans-Atlantic slave trade itself. With drinking water running perilously low for both captors and African captives alike, the ship's officers coldly determined that their human cargo represented the most expendable commodity onboard.

And so it was that over a span of several late November days, the Zong's crew began systematically throwing groups of enslaved Africans overboard into the roiling waters. The men first, followed by women and children as the mass killings mounted from 10, to 20, to eventually over 130 people murdered through drowning at sea. Their bodies left to be consumed by sharks as cost-saving measures deployed whenever ships ran short on provisions.

But while Cozens and posterity would regard the Zong massacre as a dreadful moral outrage even for its contemporary era, its ramifications would unfurl in far more unnerving ways. For upon reaching its destination of Jamaica, the ship's owners submitted a claim to their maritime insurance syndicate for the lost "cargo"; setting off a landmark lawsuit that put human ethics squarely at odds with law and capitalism's mercantile self-interest.

Britain's most respected maritime law firm of the day, Messrs. Bingham and Butterworth was retained by the ship's syndicate. Their legal arguments revolved not around the inherent barbarity of murdering innocent souls, but whether the Zong's crew had formed proper calculations to ensure tossing the captives overboard was indeed the most profitable decision.

"It was not the case of the master of a ship putting some sailors aboard on the principle of 'every one for himself,'" one of the firm's lawyers infamously argued in court. "This was the case of throwing over an excessive cargo of blacks that had rendered the ship unsafe."

That such well-regarded barristers could advocate for justifying mass murder in open court through arguments prioritizing profits over humanity laid bare the dehumanization encoded within the Trans-Atlantic slave trade and it's supporting commercial apparatus. It remains a sin hardwired into the DNA of global capitalism itself.

However, the controversial case revealed not only the human toll and racial subjugation inseparable from the Trans-Atlantic trade. It exposed deeper cracks in Britain's governing systems and economies that had become toxically incentivized and complicit in perpetuating atrocities on an industrial scale all in service of capitalist expediency.

While slave owners and profiteers may have been the most obvious villains, the real root evil persisted in bureaucratic, legal and commercial institutions corrupted to provide sanitized alibis for human plunder.

Two centuries on, the legacy of the Zong's horror still radiates across the African diaspora and demands for atonement remain unresolved and contested. In 2007, the British government issued a public apology for its failure to address the "unbearable suffering" caused by slavery sooner.

However the symbolic gesture did little to address reparation demands from Caribbean nations and advocacy groups who see the wealth of colonizers, shipping magnates and modern-day corporations as rooted in enslaved African labor.

Alwy M. Jones

Devastating Legacy of Nuclear Testing on Bikini Atoll

For over seven decades, the indigenous Marshallese people of Bikini Atoll have been embroiled in a contentious legal battle with the United States, seeking justice and compensation for the devastating impacts of nuclear weapons testing in their homeland.

In the aftermath of World War II, as the Cold War tensions escalated, the United States sought remote Pacific islands to conduct nuclear testing as part of developing an advanced atomic arsenal. In 1946, the residents of Bikini Atoll, a part of the Marshall Islands, were relocated by U.S. officials under the promise that they would be able to return home after the "brief" nuclear tests were completed. However, between 1946 and 1958, the U.S. detonated 23 nuclear devices on the atoll, including the 1954 Castle Bravo hydrogen bomb; the most powerful nuclear test conducted by the U.S. and about 1,000 times more powerful than the Hiroshima bomb. These tests vaporized islands, left behind widespread radioactive contamination, and exposed both American servicemen and the displaced Marshallese population to alarming levels of radiation.

In the ensuing decades, the Bikini islanders have engaged in an uphill legal battle against the U.S. government, demanding adequate compensation for the loss of their homeland and the long-term health impacts suffered by their community.

In the 1970s, after failed attempts to return to their contaminated islands, they accepted a lump sum payment of $6.5 million as part of a broader settlement with the U.S. However, this amount has proven woefully inadequate, failing to cover the costs of long term relocation and healthcare for radiation related illnesses. In recent years, the Marshallese government has stepped up efforts to hold the U.S. accountable, seeking additional compensation through international courts and the United Nations. Some progress has been made, with the U.S. providing $2 billion in assistance through the Compact of Free Association, but concerns remain about the long-term habitability of Bikini and other affected atolls.

Today, the Bikini islanders remain displaced, with their homes and traditional way of life irrevocably disrupted. The community continues to grapple with heightened cancer rates, birth defects, and other health issues linked to radiation exposure.

As the legal fight persists, the Bikini people are determined to ensure their plight is not forgotten, seeking acknowledgment of the immense sacrifices they endured and advocating for a comprehensive resolution that protects their human rights and restores their ancestral lands. This ongoing saga underscores the catastrophic human toll of nuclear weapons testing and the moral obligation of nations to rectify such grievous injustices inflicted upon indigenous populations in the pursuit of military dominance.

Alwy M. Jones

Historical Analysis of World War II Atrocities in Croatia During The Ustasha Regime

The Ustasha regime, led by Ante Pavelic, oversaw the establishment and operation of Catholic extermination camps during World War II, perpetrating heinous atrocities against Serbs, Jews, Romani people, and anti-fascist Croats.

Established in 1941, Jasenovac was the largest and most infamous camp. It functioned as the epicenter of systematic extermination, employing brutal methods such as mass shootings, gassing, and forced labor leading to exhaustion and death. In addition to Jasenovac, several other camps, including Stara Gradiska, were established to facilitate the mass killings and ethnic cleansing perpetrated by the Ustasha regime. The Ustasha regime was driven by an ultranationalist ideology that sought to create an ethnically pure Greater Croatia. This extremist ideology fueled the establishment and operation of the extermination camps, fostering an environment of extreme brutality and intolerance.

The Ustasha regime orchestrated the systematic genocide of Serbs, Jews, and Romani individuals, resulting in the deaths of approximately 32,000 Jews, 25,000 Romani people, and over 300,000 Serbs. These atrocities were carried out with meticulous planning and organization, leading to widespread suffering and loss of life.

The victims of the Ustasha regime suffered unimaginable horrors, enduring mass executions, torture, and forced labor. Reports of sadistic killings using hand tools and knives further underscore the extreme brutality of the camps.

The establishment of these camps occurred within the broader context of World War II, during which fascist and Nazi ideologies fueled ethnic and racial persecution across Europe. The Ustasha regime's actions were emblematic of the genocidal policies that characterized this tumultuous period in history. The Ustasha regime, under Ante Pavelic's leadership, actively implemented policies aimed at the extermination of ethnic and religious groups deemed undesirable. The establishment of the extermination camps served as a tool for the systematic execution of these abhorrent policies.

The Ustasha regime's policies had far-reaching repercussions, resulting in the decimation of entire communities and leaving a lasting legacy of trauma and loss for the victims and their descendants. The Ustasha regime's establishment and operation of Catholic extermination camps under Ante Pavelic's governance represent a harrowing chapter in the annals of World War II atrocities. The deliberate perpetration of genocide, the underpinning ideologies, and the profound impact on victims and the broader historical context underscore the gravity of the Ustasha regime's actions and their enduring significance in the collective memory of this dark period in history.

- Bodies of the Jasenovac camp prisoners in the Sava River.

- Bodies of victims of the Gudovac Massacre.

- Group of Serb civilians forcibly converted at a church in Glina.

Alwy M. Jones

St. Bartholomew's Day Massacre of 1572

The St. Bartholomew's Day Massacre was a devastating event that unfolded in Paris and other regions of France in 1572. It represented the horrific climax of decades of escalating religious tensions and violence between French Catholics and the rising Calvinist Protestant minority known as Huguenots.

By the mid-16th century, the spread of Calvinism and the ideals of the Protestant Reformation had taken deep root in France, posing an existential threat to the power of the staunchly Catholic monarchy and the established Church. The Huguenots grew to comprise up to 10% of the French population, including many members of the aristocracy.

A climate of mutual fear, distrust, and hatred festered between the religious factions, periodically erupting into bouts of mob violence, assassination plots, and military clashes during the French Wars of Religion (1562-1598). Both sides committed atrocities and massacres as they vied for supremacy.

In 1572, in an effort to unite the factions through marriage, the young Huguenot king Henry of Navarre wedded Marguerite de Valois, daughter of the staunchly Catholic Queen Mother Catherine de' Medici. The marriage celebrations brought droves of prominent Huguenots to Paris.

However, court records and correspondence reveal that Catherine de' Medici, deeply distrustful of the Protestants, conspired with Catholic nobles to exterminate the heretic Huguenot leadership assembled in Paris. After an assassination attempt on a Huguenot admiral sparked violence in the streets, this set the shocking massacre plot in motion.

In the early hours of August 24th 1572 the feast day of St. Bartholomew, ringing church bells signaled the start of the massacres. Bands of Catholic militia and gangs proceeded to hunt down, torture, and butcher any Protestants they could find over the span of days. Prime targets were Huguenot ministers, members of the nobility, and common people of all ages.

Eyewitness accounts describe victims being hacked to death, mutilated, or flung from windows onto pikes raised by angry mobs in the streets below. Even children were not spared from the bloodshed amid chaotic scenes of unrestrained carnage.

The worst of the slaughter took place in Paris in the first three days, but the killing subsequently spread outwards to provincial towns over the following weeks as the monarchy issued orders to kill remaining Protestants nationwide.

By the time the massacres finally ended in October, it is estimated that at least 10,000 French Protestants had been slain across the country. The St. Bartholomew's Day atrocities represented not only a human tragedy of grisly proportions, but effectively destroyed any remaining hopes for a religious co-existence in France.

The massacres turned the once fruitful French Renaissance into an extended cycle of retaliatory religious warfare and instability that would last until the Edict of Nantes in 1598. Trust between Protestants and Catholics had been permanently shattered.

More broadly, news of the massacres in Paris sparked outrage and shockwaves across Europe. It galvanized the Protestant world to view Catholic France as a treacherous enemy to their religion. This hardened confessional battle lines across the continent during a period when different Christian denominations were struggling to co-exist within the same nations.

The St. Bartholomew's Day Massacre exemplified the fearsome depths of religious hatred, violence, and depravity that early modern states were willing to embrace to impose spiritual and political uniformity on their populations. It demonstrated how paranoia, polarization, and a climate of existential dread could rapidly escalate into one of the worst instances of faith-based bloodletting prior to the 20th century.

Historians view this event as a pivotal turning point that exacerbated Christian sectarian conflicts for generations and exposed the fragility of religious tolerance even in a nation celebrated for its Renaissance achievements. It has endured as a nightmarish touchstone for how quickly threats to ruling powers, real or imagined, could descend into unspeakable acts of brutality and murder all in the name of religious conviction.

Alwy M. Jones

Bengal Famine of 1943

The Bengal famine of 1943 was one of the greatest humanitarian crises of World War II and a tragic chapter in the history of British colonial rule in India. Winston Churchill, as the Prime Minister of the United Kingdom during this period, played a central role in policies and decision-making that exacerbated the suffering of millions of Bengalis.

In 1943, a combination of factors, including wartime disruptions to food supplies, the seizure of rice stocks for military purposes, and devastating cyclones and fungal diseases that destroyed crops, led to a catastrophic shortage of food in Bengal. Despite repeated warnings from colonial officials about the impending famine, Churchill's government was slow to respond and prioritized the needs of the war effort over relief efforts.

Churchill's actions, or rather inactions, during the Bengal famine were shaped by a complex interplay of factors, including his strategic priorities, racial biases, and a lack of understanding of the severity of the crisis. He prioritized the diversion of food and resources to support the British war effort in Europe and other theaters, even as the situation in Bengal deteriorated rapidly.

Churchill's government also rejected offers of food aid from other countries and blocked attempts by colonial officials to use the surplus rice stocks from Burma to alleviate the famine. Additionally, his notorious remarks, such as dismissing the famine as a "bogy" and questioning why Gandhi hadn't died yet, revealed a callous disregard for the suffering of the Bengali population.

The consequences of Churchill's policies were catastrophic. Estimates suggest that between 2 and 3 million Bengalis perished from starvation, malnutrition, and related diseases during the famine. Scenes of emaciated bodies lying in the streets, families resorting to desperate measures to survive, and widespread social upheaval were etched into the collective memory of the region.

The famine not only claimed millions of lives but also had far reaching political ramifications. It fueled resentment against British colonial rule and contributed to the growing momentum for Indian independence. The British government's perceived indifference to the suffering of its colonial subjects eroded its moral authority and legitimacy in the eyes of many Indians.

The Bengal famine of 1943 has left an indelible mark on Churchill's legacy as a wartime leader. While he is widely celebrated for his leadership during World War II, his handling of the Bengal crisis has been a subject of intense scrutiny and criticism from historians and scholars.

Critics argue that Churchill's actions, or lack thereof, during the famine were a manifestation of the racism and imperial attitudes that permeated the British colonial system. His prioritization of the war effort over the lives of millions of Indians has been viewed as a stark illustration of the dehumanizing effects of colonialism and the disregard for the well-being of colonial subjects.

However, some historians have also argued that Churchill's actions were shaped by the exigencies of wartime and that his primary focus was on winning the war against the Axis powers. They contend that while his decisions were undoubtedly tragic, they were not necessarily motivated by racial prejudice or a deliberate policy of neglect.

The Bengal famine of 1943 remains a poignant reminder of the human cost of colonialism and the complex legacy of Winston Churchill's leadership. It has sparked debates about the ethical responsibilities of governments during times of crisis and the enduring impact of historical events on contemporary perceptions of leaders and nations.

In conclusion, the Bengal famine of 1943 was a catastrophic event that exposed the harsh realities of British colonial rule in India and the often conflicting priorities of wartime leadership. Churchill's actions, or lack thereof, during this crisis have left an indelible mark on his legacy and continue to shape our understanding of the complexities of colonial history and the human toll of political decision-making.

- Bengal famine of 1943: Dead and dying children on a Calcutta street published in the Statesman 22 August 1943.

- A family on the sidewalk in Calcutta during the Bengal famine of 1943.

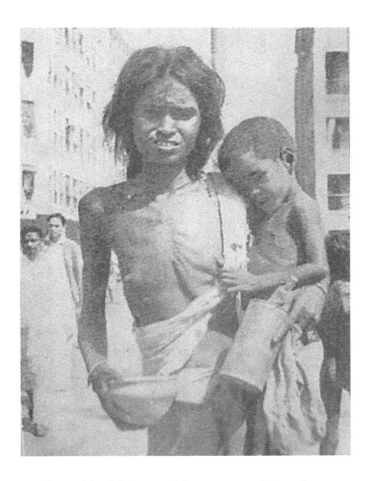

- Mother with child on a Calcutta street. Bengal famine 1943.

- Orphans who survived the famine.

Alwy M. Jones

The Tragic Death of Marwa El-Sherbini

The brutal slaying of Marwa El-Sherbini has reverberated across the globe, igniting outrage over issues of hate crimes, Islamophobia and access to justice for minority communities. The 31-year-old Egyptian woman was stabbed 18 times in front of her young son inside a Dresden courtroom on July 1st 2009, by a German man with anti-Muslim leanings whom she was set to testify against.

For many in the Islamic world, El-Sherbini's killing epitomized the dangers faced by visibly Muslim women who endure discrimination, harassment and violence because of their religious beliefs. She died simply for wearing a headscarf. Protests and vigils denouncing her murder erupted across Egypt, Turkey, Iraq and other Muslim majority nations.

The circumstances surrounding El-Sherbini's death were particularly abhorrent to human rights groups. She was in the courtroom to provide testimony against her eventual killer, Alexander Wiens, who had hurled racist abuse and insulted her for wearing an Islamic headscarf during a public encounter in 2008. When she moved to defend herself from his verbal harassment, he resorted to physical violence that left her with a traumatic injury requiring over a month of hospitalization.

Yet in the retrial a year later, as El-Sherbini calmly took the stand to offer her account of that original incident, Alexander Wiens charged at her with a knife from the courtroom gallery. Despite her pleas for help, he repeatedly plunged the blade into El-Sherbini's 31week pregnant body as her 3 year-old son looked on helplessly. The court security officers were too late to stop the attack.

This was a lethal act of hate against a Muslim woman for defending herself from bigotry. It illustrated how easily Islamophobia can escalate into deadly violence against innocent people.

There was also criticism of German authorities for potentially mishandling El-Sherbini's initial harassment case a year prior. Some questioned whether more could have been done to take her original complaint seriously and prevent this subsequent tragedy.

The legal fallout following El-Sherbini's murder saw Alexander Wiens convicted of murder and hate crimes, receiving the maximum life sentence. But for many in the global Muslim diaspora, her needless death exemplified how even in modern, liberal societies, institutional biases and an undercurrent of anti-Muslim bigotry can have devastating, if not deadly, consequences.

Alwy M. Jones

Cologne Muslim Community Still Reeling 15 Years after Hate Attack

It's been nearly over two decades since a powerful nail bomb ripped through the Turkish Islamic Union for Religious Affairs building, injuring 22 people. But for the city's Muslim community, the physical and psychological scars of that hateful act linger as a painful reminder of the prejudices they continue to face.

On a warm June evening in 2004, the two story community center was filled with nearly 40 people attending religious studies and Quran lessons. At around 9pm, a blast from the homemade explosive device tore through the building's entrance, shrapnel lacerating victims with nails and debris. Four people were seriously wounded, including the wife of the center's imam who was blinded in one eye.

Law enforcement quickly determined the bombing was an act of anti-Muslim hatred aimed at intimidating Germany's large Turkish minority population. The suspects were tied to the neo-Nazi National Socialist Underground group.

In the aftermath, Muslim leaders denounced the attack as an assault not just on their community, but on Germany's fundamental values of religious freedom and diversity. They channeled anger into advocacy, demanding authorities take stronger action to curb racism and far-right extremism.

A 2017 study found that Muslims in Germany face disproportionate levels of hate crimes, discrimination in housing and employment, along with mounting Islamophobia rhetoric from fringe political parties. Anti-racism advocates argue more must be done through education, law enforcement and civic engagement to promote better integration and de-radicalization efforts.

At the Turkish-Islamic Union center, the damage from the bomb has been fully repaired. But reminders are still visible, from commemorative plaques to enhanced security features installed in the wake of the attack.

As Germany grapples with its fraught history of xenophobia, anti-immigrant violence and the resurgence of emboldened far-right factions, the Cologne bombing endures as a tragic symbol of religious intolerance and an unheeded warning of the hatred that festers when it goes unchallenged.

Alwy M. Jones

The Enduring Toll of Balbir Singh Sodhi's Murder

It was a Saturday morning, just four days after the September 11th attacks, when Balbir Singh Sodhi was gunned down in front of the Chevron gas station he owned and operated. The 49 year old Sikh American was murdered in a vile act driven by hate, backlash and ignorance in the aftermath of 9/11.

Sodhi, who wore a turban and had a beard in adherence with his Sikh faith, was mistaken for an Arab Muslim by his killer 42 year old Frank Silva Roque, a self-proclaimed "patriot" seeking to lash out at those he blamed for the terror attacks. Roque fired multiple shots at Sodhi from close range as the immigrant from India planted landscape seedlings outside his business.

In those frightening days and weeks after 9/11, when security fears ran rampant, Balbir Singh Sodhi's murder sent shockwaves through communities of Sikhs, Muslims, Arabs and other minority groups suddenly being targeted and vilified solely for their appearance.

Advocacy organizations like the Sikh Coalition tracked a spike in hate crimes and discrimination aimed at Sikhs in the aftermath. They rallied to raise awareness of their distinct 500 year old religious identity, different from Muslims, Arabs or the 9/11 perpetrators.

But progress was slow, with reports of schoolyard bullying, workplace harassment, violent assaults and even another deadly attack on a Sikh man in Seattle in 2017; 16 years after Balbir Singh Sodhi's killing. His murder shattered a sense of security for many Sikh Americans who thought generational barriers of ignorance and bias had gradually dissipated. Yet the trauma endures, especially for youth traumatized by hate at a young age. Several non-profit groups have emerged teaching youth how to cope with bias, appreciate their heritage, and serve as ambassadors of their Sikh identity.

At a memorial marking the 20th anniversary of his death in 2021, Balbir Singh Sodhi was remembered as a pioneering voice of unity, the first widely reported casualty of an anti-Muslim, anti-Sikh, and anti-immigrant furor inadvertently triggered by 9/11. His killing forced an uncomfortable reckoning of the prejudices and lack of religious literacy still rippling through American society.

Alwy M. Jones

Zurich Mosque Shooting Shatters Swiss Haven of Tolerance

This picturesque Swiss city has long prided itself on being a bastion of peace, prosperity and progressive values. A place where people from all backgrounds could live harmoniously side-by-side.

But that idyllic sense of security was brutally shattered in the early evening of December 19th 2016, when a gunman stormed the Islamic Center of Zurich during evening prayers and opened fire.

The attack left three worshippers wounded; two Somali migrants aged 28 and 32, and a 54-year-old Swiss man who would later succumb to his injuries. Over 20 rounds were fired into the prayer hall before the assailant fled, leaving a scene of chaos, blood and unfathomable terror.

While the motive is still disputed, authorities swiftly labeled the assault an apparent terrorist attack motivated by violent extremist ideology and hatred of Muslims. The suspect, a 24 year old Swiss man with a history of neo-Nazi ties, was arrested outside his home later that evening.

For the city's Muslim population, estimated at over 30,000, the carnage at their beloved house of worship represented a sickening violation of their fundamental rights to security and religious freedom.

In the days after, Muslim community members grappled with a profound sense of vulnerability along with fears over potential backlash or retaliation from a climate of growing xenophobia across Europe amid the refugee crisis.

Yet they took solace and strength in the outpouring of solidarity from fellow Zurich residents and Swiss officials strongly reaffirming their constitutional commitment to inclusion and non-discrimination. Outside the Islamic Center, a makeshift memorial emerged with piles of flowers, hand-written notes and countless tea lights, a poignant symbol of comfort and unity.

While local and federal authorities have made efforts to enhance security at Muslim centers and other minority institutions, the traumatic impact of the Zurich shooting lingers heavily.

At the same time, Muslim youth leaders have intensified efforts to build bridges across cultural divides through school outreach programs, open houses and advocacy campaigns designed to combat hateful stereotyping or rhetoric that could enable further radicalization.

Alwy M. Jones

The Iran Air Flight 655 Disaster

On the morning of July 3rd 1988, Iran Air Flight 655 took off from Bandar Abbas International Airport bound for Dubai. The Airbus A300 passenger jet was carrying 290 people, including 66 children. But this routine short-haul flight across the Persian Gulf would end in unthinkable horror.

Cruising at over 600 mph and an altitude just shy of 14,000 feet, the Iranian airliner was just 8 miles off the coast of Iran when the unimaginable occurred. The United States Navy guided missile cruiser USS Vincennes unleashed two SM-2MR surface-to-air missiles, blasting the civilian airplane out of the sky.

Within moments, the Flight 655 wreckage plunged into the Gulf's choppy waters as fiery debris rained down on small Iranian shipping boats below. Every one of the 290 civilians aboard perished in the tragedy. It was later revealed to be a horrific case of "misidentified target", the Vincennes crew wrongly mistook the routine commercial jet for an Iranian F-14 fighter.

The shoot down occurred at the height of the Iran-Iraq War with tensions running high in the strategic Strait of Hormuz after the US Navy guided missile frigate USS Samuel B. Roberts struck an Iranian mine two months earlier. It set the stage for a series of tit-for-tat strikes between US and Iranian forces that pushed the region to the brink of wider conflict.

When smoke cleared on that fateful July day, the Flight 655 catastrophe stood as one of the worst disasters in commercial aviation history.

For the grieving families of victims spanning 6 nations, along with enraged Iranian citizens, the incident represented an unconscionable act of aggression by American military forces. Protests erupted across Iran's major cities, further inflaming the revolutionary regime's hostilities toward the U.S. "Great Satan."

Within 24 hours, President Reagan scrambled to express remorse and "deep regret" publicly without admitting direct wrongdoing by the U.S. An official government investigation followed, scrutinizing technological failures and flawed procedures by the Vincennes crew in the intense sea skirmish.

The report found fatefully that the commercial airliner was mistaken for an Iranian F-14 fighter via deficient radar equipment in the heat of battle. But it also uncovered shocking, broader lapses in operational training along with tense, poor communication between the Vincennes commanding officers amid the unfolding crisis situation before launching their missiles.

In 1996, the governments of Iran and the United States reached a settlement awarding $61.8 million in compensation to the victim families. Yet the matter stands anything but resolved to this day. Iran has continually protested that settlement as "a tiny pittance" that does not reflect the gravity of such a catastrophic loss of civilian life through U.S. incompetence and negligence.

Yet 35 years on, the destroyed Airbus wreckage remains buried deep beneath the Persian Gulf's dark waters, a haunting tomb and symbol of the accidental devastation caused when the "fog of war" becomes a blinding tragedy of errors. As one Iranian military officer who lost his wife on Flight 655 bitterly remarked, "The plane's debris is still there because America never really accepted responsibility."

Alwy M. Jones

France's Contentious Legacies in West Africa's Anti-Terror Fight

Across the swaths of the Sahel and West Africa, a devastating arc of insecurity has taken hold. Emboldened extremist groups like Al-Qaeda affiliates and Boko Haram have unleashed a relentless campaign of violence, displacing millions and destabilizing an already fragile region.

As the human toll and geopolitical risks continue to mount, accusations are growing louder that France, the former colonial power with expansive economic interests and military presence in its one-time African territories has played an inadvertent if not complicit role in allowing the terrorism crisis to metastasize.

France has a long history of sowing chaos through its self-serving policies aimed at maintaining influence in the region at all costs. Its actions laid the kindling that terrorist groups then lit on fire.

The criticism stems from legacies dating back to the post-colonial period. Skeptics argue that for decades, the French propped up a succession of authoritarian leaders who subjugated ethnic minorities and inflamed resentments that later gave rise to breakaway extremist movements. France is also accused of prioritizing extraction of the region's immense natural resources over promoting equitable development.

Paris's more recent military interventions like Operation Serval in Mali in 2013 temporarily suppressed the terrorist threat but created power vacuums exploited by other non-state armed groups. Tensions remain over whether France's counterterrorism tactics, which included occasional air strikes and arming local militias, indiscriminately impacted civilian populations.

How U.S. Interventions Undermined Democracy in Latin America

From Guatemala to Chile, Washington's determination to aggressively oppose leftist movements and install amenable regimes left a trail of upheaval, human rights abuses and enduring mistrust across the Western Hemisphere throughout the Cold War era.

Perhaps no example better exemplifies the hardline U.S. stance than the 1954 coup in Guatemala overthrowing the democratically elected president Jacobo Arbenz. His reforms aimed at empowering the peasantry and nationalization of the U.S. owned United Fruit Company aroused intense fears in Washington over potential communist influences, despite Arbenz's democratically center-left policies.

Authorized by President Eisenhower and engineered by the CIA, the covert operation replaced Arbenz with the military dictatorship of Carlos Castillo Armas through arms distributions and propaganda campaigns to foment regime change. It marked the beginning of over 30 years of bloody civil war and human rights catastrophes in the impoverished Central American nation.

It confirmed that no democracy would truly be tolerated in Guatemala if it didn't toe the American line. It sent a chilling message of brutal repression of legitimate reform movements.

The same pattern repeated across the hemisphere throughout the Cold War, as popularly elected leaders like Salvador Allende in Chile or Joao Goulart in Brazil met similarly ruthless ends through U.S. backed coups ushering in regimes under military juntas and right-wing authoritarians.

In these operations, Washington often supplemented covert political machinations with arms shipments, training of oppressive police and intelligence operations, and even direct military intervention. Few exceeded the depths of immorality as in the U.S. invasions of both the Dominican Republic in 1965 and the disastrous Bay of Pigs fiasco in Cuba in 1961, the latter an attempt at reverse regime change gone disastrously awry.

Such unilateral interventionist tactics had disastrous destabilizing effects while fundamentally betraying America's stated democratic principles. Human rights monitors documented atrocities across the juntas of U.S. installed regimes; massacres, torture, "disappearances" and scorched-earth tactics against dissidents and indigenous populations.

The Guatemalan civil war alone saw over 200,000 killed, mostly indigenous Maya people. In Argentina's "Dirty War" under the U.S. backed junta, estimates of those "disappeared" range from 10,000 to 30,000. And in El Salvador in 1981, the Reagan administration doubled down on supplying the military that later massacred over 800 civilians in the village of El Mozote.

The United States kept reasserting this anti-democratic ideology that only right-wing regimes were valid in Latin America regardless of how they took power; through open elections or not. It induced political trauma that undermined those nations' institutional progress for generations.

Ultimately, the United States' reflexive interventions to preserve its unipolar sphere of influence bred intense resentment and distrust of the "American imperialists" in the eyes of many. The impacts undermined U.S. credibility as the supposed "leader of the free world," while inducing long-term brain drains, economic stagnation, and cycles of civil conflicts across Latin nations in the campaigns' aftermath.

Even now from Cuba to Venezuela, some of the harshest U.S. critics and pushback against its influence emanate from nations with indelible memories of Washington's regime change tactics and enabling of brutal strongmen through overt and covert operations.

As scholar John Coatsworth concluded, "For many in Latin America, the United States was not the champion of democracy, but its principal enemy."

Alwy M. Jones

Duma Attack Survivors' Anguish Speaks to Larger Wounds in West Bank

In the pre-dawn hours of July 31st 2015, Jewish extremist settlers hurled firebombs and sprayed graffiti on the one-story home in this small village. The blaze trapped sleeping family members inside as the house became an inferno.

18 month old Ali Dawabsheh burned to death immediately in his bedroom, contaminated by deadly smoke inhalation. His mother Riham, 27, and father Saad succumbed to their wounds days later in Israeli hospitals with excruciating third degree burns covering most of their bodies. Only Ahmad, then just 4 years old, survived, though badly disfigured with burns covering 60 percent of his small body.

The attack was swiftly condemned by Palestinian and international authorities as a blatant act of terror, part of the systematic harassment and vigilante violence minority extremist Israeli settlers in the West Bank have perpetrated against Palestinians for decades. Graffiti scrawled at the scene proclaimed "Revenge" and "Long live the king messiah."

The attackers turned out to be a radical Jewish terror cell composed of extremist West Bank settlers subscribing to fringe Jewish supremacist ideologies advocating the ethnic cleansing of Arabs from the Biblical Jewish homeland. At trial, these "Hilltop Youth" showed no remorse over the Dawabsheh family killings, defending them as an integral part of their religious struggle to seize control of the entire West Bank.

While Israel's government swiftly disavowed the attack as a "terrorist" act that didn't represent its values or policies, criticism mounted over systemic impunity for perpetrators of such "price tag" retribution attacks. Human rights monitors had tracked over 200 incidents of settler violence so far that year alone, with few seeing any prosecutions. Some accuse authorities of turning a blind eye to tacitly encourage driving Palestinians off disputed lands.

Four year old Ahmad Dawabsheh remained hospitalized recovering from his critical burns while bravely learning how to walk and talk again. Images of the orphaned, scarred child became a global symbol of Palestinian suffering under the occupation, fueling outrage across the Arab world.

Alwy M. Jones

The Rage Fueling Mohammed Abu Khdeir's Brutal Killing

On the morning of July 2nd 2014, the charred remains of a 16 year old Palestinian boy were discovered in the outskirts of Jerusalem. He had been beaten and burned alive.

The victim was Mohammed Abu Khdeir, a Palestinian from the Shuafat neighborhood whose only crime was being an Arab youth in the wrong place at the wrong time amid a crucible of spiraling Israeli-Palestinian violence.

It was amid this climate of rage that Mohammed encountered the unthinkable on his way to morning prayers at a local mosque. Surveillance footage captured the teenager being forced into a car by two Israeli youths before being driven to the wooded abduction site and savagely attacked. The sheer barbarity of murdering an innocent boy exacted a collective trauma on Palestinians, including rioting and furious denunciations of Israeli aggression.

Within a week, the cross-border exchanges of rockets and airstrikes exploded into the seven week Gaza war between Israel and Hamas, a conflict fueled by the outrage from Mohammed's immolation and subsequent deadly crackdowns by Israeli troops on Palestinian protesters.

While Mohammed's killers were eventually convicted of murder and handed stiff sentences, human rights monitors expressed alarm that the long chain of impunity for hate crimes by Israeli extremists against Palestinians enabled such a horrific act of incitement to transpire. For Palestinians themselves, the grief compounded existing anxieties over systemic discrimination, oppression under occupation, and the specter of potential ethnic cleansing in parts of Jerusalem.

Alwy M. Jones

Tomb of the Patriarchs Stained by Mass Murderer's Hatred

30 years later, the scene of unspeakable carnage at one of the most sacred sites in the Holy Land continues to loom as an open wound of seared trauma.

On February 25th 1994, this ancient West Bank city housing the revered Cave of the Patriarchs was shaken by gunfire and anguished cries echoing from the Ibrahimi Mosque. In a premeditated act, the Brooklyn born Israeli settler and physician Baruch Goldstein had unleashed a hailstorm of bullets into the throngs of Muslim worshippers.

By the time Goldstein's assault rifle was finally wrestled away, he had massacred 29 Palestinian civilians and wounded over 100 more; their blood pooling across the ornate mosque floors as bodies convulsed in agony. Among the dead were children as young as 2 years old.

It was incomprehensible savagery at a site meant to be a unifying sanctuary for the children of Abraham, the man showed no mercy and he seemed to draw pleasure from such indiscriminate slaughter.

To outsiders, Goldstein's motives appeared rooted in an extremist Jewish ideology embracing violence and ethnic cleansing to establish a "Greater Israel" comprising the entire Biblical land of Judea and Samaria. As a resident of the renegade Kiyrat Arba settlement in Hebron, the murderous doctor had nursed a virulent hatred of Arabs and Muslims.

He saw Arabs as sub-human contaminants that needed to be purged from the Patriarchs' holy tomb and all the occupied territories.

In the West Bank's tinderbox of festering resentments and religious nationalism, Goldstein's shooting represented more than a lone actor's depravity. It revealed how the Israeli settler movement's most militant fringes enabled through state supported land seizures and lax security oversight had embraced an eliminationism theology dangerously reminiscent of historical ethnic supremacists.

The massacre triggered immediate fury and reprisal attacks throughout the Palestinian territories before Israeli security forces intervened to restore a tenuous calm. Goldstein was ultimately beaten to death by survivors at the scene.

In the aftermath, both Israeli and Palestinian authorities condemned the rampage as an act of terror and promised decisive action to prevent any recurrences. But nearly three decades later, with the issues of settlements, security and self-governance still unresolved, the Patriarchs' Tomb and all of Hebron remain a potential arena of discord, its Mosque still riddled with bullet holes.

While some called for Goldstein's remains to be exhumed, he still lies interred within the enclave of Kiyrat Arba. A memorial condemning him as a "vile terrorist" rises only meters away from his grave's plaque hailing him as a "revered doctor and saint." The contradictory tributes encapsulate a dark truth

Alwy M. Jones

that for every worshipper seeking faith at the ancient Tomb, a dangerous fringe still rationalizes unthinkable hatred as sanctioned piety.

Alwy M. Jones

How France's Hegemonic Shadows Still Loom Over Its Former Colonies

From the blistering deserts of its West African realms to the lush islands of the Caribbean and Pacific, France's colonial empire was once vast, sprawling over millions of square miles and subjugating tens of millions of indigenous peoples. While that era has ended, a newly critical examination reveals how the tentacles of French hegemony have persisted, economically, politically and culturally complicating the path to true sovereignty for its former colonies.

For decades after achieving independence, most former French colonies maintained the CFA franc currency, whose values and monetary policies were centralized under French control. Critics have long argued this effective financial suzerainty allowed France to manipulate economies to favor its corporations' extraction and exploitation of resources like minerals, oil, cocoa and cotton with minimal domestic reinvestment.

To this day, France retains military bases, forces and defense pacts across its former colonial territories; from Djibouti to New Caledonia. While officials frame this presence as essential security cooperation, it has allowed Paris to readily intervene in the internal affairs of these nations when its geopolitical interests are perceived to be at stake. Examples range from supporting authoritarian regimes to waging the War in Mali against Islamist insurgencies.

More insidious, however, has been France's "language privilege"; the perpetuated primacy and imposition of French language in all aspects of national life in its former colonies. From schools to media to government administration, indigenous languages like Arabic, Wolof and Khmer were suppressed and derided in favor of French linguistic dominance. While now gradually reversing, this cultural imperialism created generational divides as native tongues were diminished as backwards.

Yet the undercurrent remains, for every French assertion of a well-intentioned "civilizing mission" bestowed upon its former colonial possessions, there are countless counterpoints: the devastating resource exploitation, the toppled democratic governments, the stifled indigenous voices. One need only glimpse the wealth disparities that persist between France and nearly all of its former colonies today.

As formerly colonized populations continue reasserting their cultural identities, languages and economic self-determination, France's hegemonic vestiges face an existential reckoning. Whether a new era of neocolonialism or genuine multiculturalism emerges remains to be seen. But those former subjects subjugated under French dominion deserve full liberation after centuries of sacrifice.

Alwy M. Jones

Unraveling the CIA's Sinister Role in Lumumba's Demise

When the Democratic Republic of Congo achieved independence from Belgium in 1960 after decades of brutal colonial rule, a wave of optimism swept across Africa. At its crest was the 34 year old firebrand Patrice Lumumba, the nation's first democratically elected prime minister and a standard-bearer for African liberation and unity.

But within a year, Lumumba had been ousted in a military coup, arrested, brutally beaten and finally executed by a firing squad under shadowy circumstances. His body was dissolving in acid to prevent a burial site from being venerated. The hopes of an independent, socialist Congo led by the charismatic nationalist died with Lumumba in that grim scene.

In the six decades since, a darkening cloud of Evidence has accumulated, implicating the U.S. government and the CIA specifically in a clandestine plot to permanently silence Lumumba and his defiant vision of a "United States of Africa" free of Western domination.

In the tense crucible of the Cold War, Congo's geostrategic position and mineral riches were pivotal. When Lumumba embraced Soviet support and started nationalizing foreign mining assets, he was seen as an existential threat to American corporate hegemony on the continent.

The CIA is known to have swiftly launched covert operations to destabilize Lumumba's government, authorizing $100,000 for that purpose, a huge sum at the time. They recruited his opponents, manipulated pro-Western Congolese rivals like Mobutu Sese Seko, and created a climate for his eventual physical demise after being captured.

While no "smoking gun" directly ties the CIA's hand to the killing itself, credible sources claim American operatives provided resources, funding and tacit approval to Lumumba's Belgian and Congolese executioners. Former CIA agents like John Stockwell have come forward with damning allegations of orchestrating the assassination.

Alwy M. Jones

Exposing the CIA's Unsavory Hand in Nkrumah's Downfall

In the heady years following Ghana's independence in 1957, Kwame Nkrumah stood as a towering figure of Africa's post-colonial awakening. His government's vision of Pan-African unity, socialist economics and anti-imperialist rhetoric represented an existential threat to the West's neocolonial interests on the continent.

Evidence is now mounting that the CIA played a provocative role in orchestrating Nkrumah's demise through a campaign of local recruitment, propaganda, and support for the very generals who would oust him in a coup d'etat while he traveled abroad in 1966.

Nkrumah had long been marked as a subversive thorn by American policymakers. As the Marxist liberation movements swept across Africa, his relationships with Soviet states and advocacy for a united, Soviet-allied "United States of Africa" were seen as unacceptably undermining U.S. hegemony.

Compounding fears were Nkrumah's moves to nationalize foreign corporate assets like the Volta River aluminum project. "Nkrumah was doing something right to get 'them' so mad," reflected the slain activist Malcolm X famously on his ally's anti-imperialist policies.

Through tireless investigation and several declassified documents, a disturbing trail of CIA perfidy has been uncovered regarding their operation in Ghana. It's confirmed that from 1962, millions of dollars were funneled into recruiting, arming and propagandizing segments of the Ghanaian military to spark unrest toward Nkrumah's government.

Key operatives like Howard Bane and Frank Demany have gone on record detailing their roles in this destabilization campaign. The CIA is also suspected of giving at least tacit support to the generals; namely Emmanuel Kwasi Kotoka and Akwasi Amankwa Afrifa whose 1966 coup successfully seized power from Nkrumah. State Department officials have maintained the CIA's activities were limited to intelligence gathering.

However, in 1978, the former CIA Station Chief in Ghana, Howard Banden, dropped a bombshell testimony alleging the Agency's active involvement in the coup plot. He cited requests from Washington to destabilize Nkrumah which the CIA operatives on the ground enthusiastically embraced.

For Nkrumah himself, the coup marked a soul-crushing betrayal by military compatriots he'd long trusted. Forced into exile, the beleaguered president never regained power before his 1972 death. The dream of his Ghanaian revolution was extinguished.

His ouster also represented a pivotal setback for the greater Pan-African liberation struggle. With Nkrumah neutralized, the continent saw a flood of Western corporate and military incursions as the threat of Marxist unity evaporated. Successive Ghanaian regimes became closer U.S. client states.

While Nkrumah's heroic legacy still burns bright for the continent's youth, this sordid chapter serves as yet another example of American interventionism crushing a nation's sovereign, democratic right to self-determination and non-aligned development. Ghana's people continue grappling with the long remnants of this neo-imperial meddling in their affairs over 50 years later.

Alwy M. Jones

Uncovering the CIA's Toxic Trail of African Coups

In the height of Cold War between the U.S. and Soviet Union, newly independent African nations represented not just fertile grounds for spreading democratic values or Marxist revolution, but also blank geopolitical slates to be tilted in favor of one superpower over the other through whatever means necessary.

As insidious declassified files and first-hand whistleblower accounts have shown, this often meant the CIA's covert operations apparatus was deployed to undermine or oust African leaders seen as too sympathetic to the USSR or hostile to American interests. The toxic legacy of that interventionism can be starkly seen in the tale of coups that rocked Mali, Chad, Guinea, Sudan and Burkina Faso.

Mali

Though Soviet educated Moussa Traore initially seized power in a coup against the pro-French government, he swiftly fell out of U.S. favor with his insular regime, nationalization of companies, and move towards Soviet alignment. CIA ties to the paratroopers who toppled Traore in 1968 have long been alleged, driven by Cold War fears and protecting U.S. uranium interests.

Chad

Decades of CIA meddling hollowed out this desert nation as a proxy battleground against Soviet backed Libya's incursions. From funneling arms to rebel forces to spreading propaganda, the Agency's clandestine efforts perpetuated a civil war morass from which Chad never recovered politically or economically.

Guinea

Though President Ahmed Sekou Toure died in 1984, evidence implicates the CIA in coup plots against his regime dating back to the 1960s out of fears his socialist policies could birth a Soviet satellite on Africa's west coast.

Sudan

When Sadiq al-Mahdi began reforms edging Sudan closer to Russia, the CIA moved swiftly, reportedly greenlighting and supporting a military faction led by Omar al-Bashir to oust him. This kicked off three decades of pariah dictatorship, genocide and civil wars.

Burkina Faso

The revolutionary Thomas Sankara's anti-imperialist rhetoric and policies provoked deep American ire and CIA plots to undermine his government by encouraging mutinous officers like his treacherous friend Blaise Compaore, who led the 1987 coup to murder Sankara, upending his transformation of the nation. Rumors swirl the CIA may again have played a hand in January 2022's coup.

Of course, unraveling the truth behind the CIA's role in decades old coups is intrinsically challenging and shrouded in plausible deniability. Many records remain classified. Yet the fingerprints of American interventionism are unmistakable from caches of declassified CIA communications and operatives' own memoirs, to the litter of ruined economies and puppet regimes the continent was saddled with for decades.

These nations suffered seismic reversals of democratic processes, economic calamity and insecurity that lingers to this day. The full truth may never be uncovered, but one pattern is clear: the Cold War battles fought over African nations by the U.S. and USSR led to a toxic legacy still poisoning the continent's progress and self-determination over half a century later.

Alwy M. Jones

Exposing France's Poisonous 'Operation Persil' in Guinea

When the West African nation of Guinea celebrated its hard won independence from French colonial rule in 1958, it represented a potent symbol of the new wave of African liberation sweeping the continent. But Paris was unwilling to simply let go of its former possession under the defiant leadership of President Ahmed Sekou Toure.

Enter Operation Persil; French Intelligence's still largely uncovered campaign to punish Toure's nationalist government through economic warfare, psychological operations, and fomenting civil unrest in hopes of reasserting control.

Toure's policies marked him as an adversary to France from the outset. His rejection of continued French economic domination and efforts to rapidly Guineanise the civil service, military, and education system represented an existential threat to the neo-colonial status quo desired by Paris.

Worse still in French eyes, Toure embraced support from the Soviet bloc, establishing close ties with the U.S.S.R. and other socialist nations a poisoned well to the staunchly anti-communist French. "He's our Fidel Castro in Africa," one French diplomat fumed of the Guinean leader to Washington.

To punish this perceived insolence and force Toure from power, France initiated an intense campaign of overt economic sabotage, suddenly terminating all assistance, withdrawing French personnel from vital infrastructure like rail lines, and even attempting to crash Guinea's fledgling currency.

However, declassified French intelligence files and whistleblower accounts reveal the far dirtier covert dimensions of Operation Persil. French operatives are confirmed to have bankrolled opposition groups, staged false flag attacks, infiltrated the government, and broadcast relentless disinformation campaigns to stir unrest against Toure.

In an era before widespread telecommunications, this psychological warfare was remarkably effective spreading exaggerated tales of food shortages, violence, and even rumors Toure had been killed or ousted from power. French handlers leveraged paid Guinean agents in efforts to build anti-Toure protest momentum.

The results were years of persistent civil turmoil and division within Guinean society as Toure resorted to authoritarian measures to maintain control. Guerilla groups carried out sabotage backed by French resources. Ethnic tensions were cynically inflamed between communities.

Coup attempts in 1960 and 1976 failed to dislodge Toure, but many analysts argue Operation Persil's dark legacy permanently undermined and radicalized his government, setting the stage for repressive dictatorship rather than Guinean democracy flourishing.

Compounding the tragedy were the poverty and ruinous economic shockwaves inflicted on the Guinean people as punishment for their sovereignty by this vindictive French campaign, with effects lingering into the present day.

In the end, Operation Persil represented a vicious blueprint for neocolonial powers to punish developing nations who defied the world order. Rarely has a nation's independence been so vengefully undermined from the outset by a bitter opposition to self-determination.

While many files remain classified, the mounting evidence leaves little doubt in the shadows of this defiant African independence struggle was the unmistakable stain of French perfidy.

Alwy M. Jones

How the CIA's Callous Crusade Crushed Democracy in Guatemala

In the early 1950s, the banana republic of Guatemala was a thorn in the side of American corporate and geopolitical interests under President Arbenz's progressive reformist leadership. His agrarian policies of expropriating unused lands from companies like United Fruit to redistribute to landless peasants struck at the heart of the U.S. empire builders. Compounding fears, Arbenz's cabinet had Communists sympathizers despite his own denials of being a Soviet pawn.

For the Eisenhower administration and the Dulles brothers atop the State Department and CIA, these dynamics proved unacceptable in America's backyard during the grip of Cold War hysteria over communist expansion. Declassified documents codename the ensuing CIA campaign to topple Arbenz as Operation PBSUCCESS.

With nearly $20 million committed (over $200 million today), PBSUCCESS employed practically every trick in the Agency's regime change playbook. Exploiting the coverage of United Fruit's vast communications networks, the CIA bombarded the Guatemalan people with a relentless torrent of anti-Arbenz propaganda, misinformation, and intimidation via radio, newspapers, and pamphlet bombardments.

More overtly, CIA operatives armed, funded, and trained a counter revolutionary force led by Carlos

Castillo Armas to commit border raids, sabotage infrastructure like rail lines, and cultivate a climate of un-governability to destabilize Arbenz's regime. Agency instigators also initiated crippling nationwide strikes and even a bogus "crypto-ethnic" movement to stir indigenous communities against the government.

By mid-1954, Guatemala had descended into virtual civil war. Though Arbenz petitioned the UN and OAS for peace support, few nations were willing to challenge the U.S. sphere of influence. The former President was forced to resign on June 27th 1954 as Armas' CIA backed rebel forces closed in on Guatemala City. "The saddest day of my life," Arbenz would later lament in exile.

Arbenz's overthrow initiated over 30 years of brutal authoritarian rule and regression in Guatemala under the iron fist of CIA cultivated regimes like Armas, culminating in the genocide against Indigenous Maya peoples by American backed military juntas in the 1980s.

President Eisenhower's infamous jubilation over PBSUCCESS as a sterling demonstration of America's burgeoning covert capabilities proved horrifyingly prophetic. The CIA's coup and destabilization campaign set the mold for countless future interventions to crush perceived leftist or socialist threats to American hegemony across the Global South in decades to come.

But for the Guatemalan people, the toll was overwhelming tens of thousands murdered, economies shattered, generations robbed of freedom and opportunity. Beginning with Arbenz's ousting, CIA fingerprints can be found tracing the contours of nearly every convulsion in the nation's tragic spiral into violence, poverty, and oppression over the latter 20th century.

While the full records remain classified, testimonies from defectors like CIA alumnus Phillip Agee and archival revelations have confirmed the culpability of American interventionism behind this seminal event. For too long, Guatemalans paid the price for the CIA's crusade to insist democracy could not bloom anywhere near America's capitalist dawn.

Alwy M. Jones

The 1953 Coup Against Iran's Democratically Elected Prime Minister Mohammad Mosaddegh, Orchestrated by The CIA and MI6

The 1953 coup against Iran's democratically elected Prime Minister Mohammad Mosaddegh, orchestrated by the CIA and MI6, was a pivotal event that had far reaching consequences for Iranian history and global relations. As a historian researching this topic, it is crucial to examine the political motivations, methods employed, and the long-term implications of this covert operation.

Political Motivations:

1. Oil Nationalization: Mosaddegh's decision to nationalize Iran's oil industry, which was controlled by the British owned Anglo-Iranian Oil Company (AIOC), was a significant factor that prompted the intervention of Western intelligence agencies. The British government feared the loss of control over Iran's oil resources and the potential domino effect on other countries in the region.

2. Cold War Context: The coup against Mosaddegh was also driven by the larger geopolitical context of the Cold War. The United States and Britain viewed Mosaddegh's government as a potential threat, fearing that Iran could align itself with the Soviet Union, which had already established a sphere of influence in Eastern Europe and parts of Asia.

3. Preserving Western Interests: The coup was motivated by a desire to maintain Western influence and control over Iran, which was considered a strategic ally in the Middle East due to its oil reserves and geographic location.

Covert Operation and Methods:

The CIA and MI6 employed various covert methods to orchestrate the coup against Mosaddegh, including:

1. Propaganda Campaigns: Extensive propaganda efforts were undertaken to undermine Mosaddegh's government and portray it as unstable and susceptible to communist influence.

2. Bribery and Manipulation: Western intelligence agencies bribed Iranian politicians, military officers, and members of the clergy to turn against Mosaddegh's government and facilitate the coup.

3. Coordinated Protests and Demonstrations: The CIA and MI6 funded and organized protests and demonstrations, creating an impression of widespread public opposition to Mosaddegh's administration.

Consequences and Long-term Impact:

1. Suppression of Democracy: The overthrow of Mosaddegh's democratically elected government set a precedent for the suppression of democratic movements in Iran, paving the way for the later establishment of the autocratic Pahlavi monarchy under Mohammad Reza Pahlavi.

2. Rise of Anti-Western Sentiment: The coup fueled anti-Western sentiment in Iran, as the actions of the CIA and MI6 were seen as a blatant violation of Iranian sovereignty and a betrayal of democratic principles.

3. Strengthening of the Iranian Revolution: The 1979 Iranian Revolution, which overthrew the Pahlavi monarchy, was partly fueled by the resentment towards Western interference in Iranian affairs, stemming from the 1953 coup.

4. Strained Relations with the West: The coup had a lasting impact on Iran's relations with the United States and Britain, leading to decades of strained diplomatic ties and mistrust.

Alwy M. Jones

The CIA Backed Military Coup in Chile on September 11th 1973

The CIA backed military coup in Chile on September 11th 1973, which overthrew the democratically elected socialist president Salvador Allende and brought Augusto Pinochet to power, had a profound impact on the country's social and economic policies, particularly those related to nationalization.

Prior to the coup, Allende's government had implemented a series of far reaching reforms aimed at redistributing wealth and nationalizing key industries, including copper mining, banking, and large scale agriculture. These policies were part of Allende's vision of a "Chilean road to socialism," which sought to transition the country towards a socialist economic model through democratic and constitutional means.

The nationalization of copper, Chile's most valuable export, was a particularly contentious issue. Allende's government took control of the country's copper mines, which were previously owned by American companies such as Kennecott and Anaconda. This decision was met with fierce opposition from the United States, which viewed it as a direct threat to American economic interests in the region.

The CIA, under the directives of President Richard Nixon and National Security Advisor Henry Kissinger, began covert operations to destabilize Allende's government and create conditions for a military coup. These efforts included funding opposition groups, manipulating the media, and encouraging economic chaos through measures such as cutting off international credit and blocking Chile's access to foreign aid. The coup, led by General Augusto Pinochet and supported by the Chilean military, resulted in the overthrow of Allende's government and the installation of a military junta. Allende himself died during the coup, with the circumstances surrounding his death remaining a subject of debate.

Under Pinochet's authoritarian rule, which lasted until 1990, Chile underwent a dramatic reversal of Allende's socialist policies. The nationalized industries were privatized, and the country embraced a free market economic model championed by a group of Chilean economists known as the "Chicago Boys," who had been trained at the University of Chicago under the guidance of Milton Friedman. The impact of this reversal was far reaching. While Chile experienced economic growth and stability under Pinochet's regime, the benefits were unevenly distributed, and the country's social safety net was significantly eroded. Income inequality increased, and poverty rates remained high, particularly in urban areas.

Furthermore, the Pinochet regime was marked by widespread human rights abuses, including torture, forced disappearances, and the persecution of political opponents. Thousands of people were killed or went missing during this period, casting a long shadow over Chile's transition to democracy.

Alwy M. Jones

The Defrocked German Catholic Priest Turned Murderer

Hans Schmidt was born in Germany in 1881 joined the priesthood at a young age and was eventually assigned to St. Patrick's Old Cathedral in New York City as a Roman Catholic priest in 1909. By all outward appearances, Schmidt seemed a pious and devoted clergyman.

However, behind the vestments, a darker and more sinister psychology was at work. In 1913, Schmidt became involved with a young woman named Anna Aumuller, a housekeeper and former nun. The two began a secret affair, and Aumuller soon became pregnant with Schmidt's child.

Fearing the scandal, Schmidt convinced Aumuller to come to the rectory on September 2nd 1913. There, he hit her with a hammer and strangled her with a rope. He then decapitated her body and disposed of the remains, including the unborn child, in a river.

The grisly murder was discovered when Anna's torso washed up on the banks weeks later. An investigation quickly centered on Schmidt as the prime suspect. When confronted, he shockingly confessed to the "ritual sacrifice," claiming he had been commanded by voices and visions to kill as an "offering of atonement."

Further examination of Schmidt's history uncovered a pattern of potential sexual assaults and improprieties with other women over the years, leading some to believe he may have been a serial predator and killer operating under a cloak of faith.

In 1914, Schmidt was tried and convicted of Anna Aumuller's murder. He was spared the death penalty but sentenced to life in prison, where he eventually died in 1947 after decades incarcerated.

Alwy M. Jones

From Embezzlement to Alleged Double Homicide

In the peaceful seaside community of Saco, a dark cloud of distrust and betrayal hung over the congregation of the local Pentecostal church in the late 20th century. At the center was their own minister, John Nelson, who went from being a purported man of God to an accused con man and eventually an alleged double murderer.

Nelson's troubles began in the 1980s while he was the pastor of the Saco Pentecostal Church. Congregants grew suspicious over apparent financial irregularities, funds that had seemingly gone missing from church coffers. An internal investigation soon uncovered Nelson's stunning breach of faith and trust.

According to court documents, Nelson had systematically embezzled thousands of dollars in church donations and funds over several years to pay for personal expenses and luxuries like cars and vacations. He reportedly engaged in complex maneuvers like money laundering to cover his trail.

Nelson was eventually convicted on theft and tax evasion charges related to the embezzlement in 1989 and served 28 months in federal prison. But this would merely be the start of even more sordid allegations against the fallen preacher. After his release from prison in the early 1990s, Nelson maintained a low profile by getting work as a self-employed handyman and construction worker in the

Saco area. That all changed in 1995 when two bodies were discovered under mysterious circumstances.

The victims were Nelson's former handyman colleagues, Paul Crowley and Danny Parker, who had both been partners in his construction business. Autopsies revealed they had been strangled or choked to death, with Nelson quickly identified as the prime suspect after his truck and belongings were found near the bodies.

Prosecutors believe the double homicides may have been motivated by a financial dispute gone violent between the former co-workers. Crowley and Parker allegedly owed Nelson money from prior construction jobs. "Nelson simply took brutal matters into his own hands when he couldn't get paid," one investigator theorized.

When the high profile double murder case ultimately went to trial in York County court in 1997, it dredged up the full sordid history of Nelson's alleged deceit, violence and ungodly misdeeds. The defense attempted to poke holes in the highly circumstantial physical evidence tying him to the victims' deaths, but the jury didn't buy it.

Nelson was convicted on two counts of murder and received two life sentences, finally being held accountable for the ultimate abuse of the authority once vested in him as a minister. "He defiled his covenant with the church and with God by showing his true greedy, sinful and violent nature," the prosecutor declared after the guilty verdict.

Today, Nelson remains imprisoned in Maine, a coda of justice for the preacher who went from purported Gospel teachings to swindling, murder and a permanent legacy as a wolf among his own flock. His name is uttered in Saco as a shameful caveat about the cloaks evil can conceal itself in, even the most holy of them.

Alwy M. Jones

Gleb Grozovsky and The Greek Orthodox Church's Darkest Scandal

In a case that has rocked the foundations of the Greek Orthodox Church and its adherents worldwide, a high ranking church official accused of not only covering up horrific acts of child sexual abuse, but fleeing justice to avoid prosecution. Gleb Grozovsky, whose despicable actions represent a profound betrayal of his position and the faith's most sacred principles.

At the center of this sordid affair is Father Vadim Abramov, a priest who used his position at youth camps operated by the Greek Orthodox Archdiocese of Russia to prey upon and violate dozens of children in unimaginably cruel ways over a period of years. According to court testimony, his acts included violent sexual assaults, physical torture, even forcing youths to reenact satanic rituals.

When allegations by some of the abused first came to light, they were instantly suppressed and covered up by higher church authorities. That's where the damning role of Gleb Grozovsky took shape.

As Chief Legal Counsellor of the Archdiocese, Grozovsky not only knew about Abramov's depravities but was instrumental in obstructing justice and allowing him to escape prosecution, all to ostensibly "protect the church's reputation." Grozovsky used his position to intimidate victims, discredit accusations, and ultimately arrange for the predator priest's transfer to another diocese where the abuse continued unabated.

When He was finally apprehended by Russian authorities in 2021 thanks to mounting evidence and pressure from victims' families, Father Abramov was tried, convicted and sentenced to 17 years in prison for his innumerable crimes against children.

However, many questioned why Grozovsky himself had not been arrested and prosecuted as an accomplice. It soon became clear that the nefarious legal advisor had one final, desperate trick to evade responsibility; fleeing to ISRAEL.

Sources indicate Grozovsky was tipped off by church contacts about an imminent arrest in Russia. Using a false identity and a clandestine smuggling operation run by sympathizers, he managed to reach ISRAELI soil where he remains in hiding to this day under the Law of Return policy for Jewish individuals.

Alwy M. Jones

Allegations of Child Rape and Abuse by the Russian Orthodox Church

In a shocking set of allegations that sent shockwaves through the Russian Orthodox Church, a senior cleric stands accused of the unthinkable; the rape and sexual abuse of at least seven children over a span of years. Archpriest Nikolai Stremsky, a highly respected figure within the Moscow Patriarchate, the governing body of the church.

According to multiple sources who have filed official reports with church authorities and law enforcement, Stremsky sexually assaulted at least seven children, some as young as six years old, while he was serving at churches in the Moscow region between 2012 and 2020. The victims included both boys and girls from families who belonged to his parish communities.

Testimony from the families describes a pattern of Stremsky grooming and luring children with gifts and favoritism, only to subject them to depraved acts of molestation and rape, often on church grounds. One survivor, now an adult, recounts psychological torment and being forced to perform sexual acts on Stremsky in exchange for "blessings."

What makes this case particularly egregious are the allegations that church officials were made aware of Stremsky's misconduct as early as 2019 but failed to act decisively. It wasn't until public pressure from a Russian social media campaign began mounting in late 2020 that the Moscow Patriarchate acknowledged it was investigating "reports of misbehavior" against the archpriest.

Since then, protests and outrage have only grown more fevered, with many demanding harsh punishment and a thorough external inquiry into potential cover-ups or enablers within church leadership. Several parishes have threatened to break away entirely if the Moscow Patriarchate does not demonstrate full accountability.

For its part, the Moscow Patriarchate issued limited statements confirming an ongoing canonical court proceedings against Stremsky, who remains suspended from priestly duties. However, specifics remain scant beyond a vague acknowledgment of "allegations of sexual misconduct involving minors."

Many see this tepid response as emblematic of a systematic culture of covering up abuse scandals plaguing the Russian Orthodox Church. There are demands for an independent secular inquiry to eliminate any possibility of bias or brushing incidents under the rug.

Based on history, the church cannot be trusted to police itself on such crimes against children, only a transparent legal process can begin delivering justice and healing.

Alwy M. Jones

Uncovering Decades of Sexual Abuse by Boston Area Rogue Monks

In a horrifying saga of violated faith and trust, a breakaway Orthodox monastic community in an affluent Boston suburb allegedly harbored a dark secret for decades, a concealed history of systemic child sexual abuse by a staggering number of monks against an untold number of victims.

As a joint investigation by local authorities and the national Orthodox Church in America (OCA) continues unraveling the full extent of the depravity, the initial findings were nothing short of catastrophic. At least 20 monks from the St. Awdry's Skete monastery face allegations ranging from fondling and molestation to outright rape against children as young as 8 years old over the past 40 years.

The levels of deceit and evil perpetrated by spiritual figures entrusted with the community's utmost faith and protection of the innocent are simply staggering, Awdry's represented the depths of Gehenna cloaked behind monastic robes and crucifixes.

Founded in 1977 by a breakaway sect of ultra-traditional Russian Orthodox hardliners, Awdry's Skete carved out an isolated existence within an upscale Brookline neighborhood. Its cluster of residential buildings operated under the guise of a monastic intentional community open to Sunday services and religious education classes for local adherents' children.

It was this steady stream of youths from the parish allegedly supplying a pool of potential victims to the monastery's predators. According to harrowing court testimonies from adult survivors, the child abuse associated with Awdry's was coordinated and systemic for decades with various monks "taking turns" victimizing kids lured under abusive disciplinary pretext. What played out behind those walls was a generational cycle of grooming, shaming, and traumatizing scores of innocent lives in the most unnatural of ways.

As despicable as the acts were, authorities are also tracking evidence that past allegations of sexual misconduct against Awdry's were actively covered up or disregarded by Orthodox authorities.

Multiple former parishioners have come forward claiming they brought reports of abuse, unusual child supervision practices and monk improprieties to hierarchs at the main OCA diocese in Syracuse, NY in the late 1990s and early 2000s. However, these claims were either dismissed or simply never investigated properly.

Alwy M. Jones

Orthodox Church Rudnevo, Moscow

In 2008, the quiet Moscow suburb of Rudnevo was rocked by a horrific case of betrayed faith and depraved criminality from an unlikely source; an Orthodox Christian priest tasked with spiritual guidance of the town's youth.

Father Grigory Krivinov stood accused of sexually assaulting at least 30 teenage boys over a span of years, exploiting his position to gain trust and prey upon the vulnerable in unconscionable ways. However, it was his final act of depravity that represented a new abysmal low.

According to court records, in fall 2008 Krivinov coerced one of his male victims, just 14 years old, into raping a stray cat while several other teenage boys filmed the debasement with mobile phones. This grotesque culmination of months of victimization shed light on the full depths of his psychological torment and disregard for innocence.

Krivinov's web of manipulation and abuse worked on many sick levels; physical, emotional, sexual and even extending into realms of ritualistic humiliation. His survivors endured compounded traumas bordering on complete dissociation from human decency.

While the cat's ultimate fate remains unknown, sources indicate Krivinov's blatant recordings of his crimes were an attempted intimidation tactic used to reinforce his dominance. Some viewed it as a grim sign the priest may have harbored ambitions of creating and distributing child sexual abuse materials.

It took months for word of Krivinov's serial predations and immoral proclivities toward bestiality to reach authorities, hampered by institutional factors. "Once involved with Krivinov's group, the kids were effectively isolated and subjected to intense victim shaming," said investigator Sasha Panova. "The church leaders' insularity also gave him ample opportunity to operate in the shadows."

When a paper trail of explicit text messages and recordings finally surfaced in late 2008, detectives swiftly made arrests, removing Krivinov and several young accomplices from an active abuse environment. Yet many assert inaction and preparatory groundwork for potential trials and diversions began emerging far earlier within ecclesiastical channels.

Signs of improper conduct and boundary violations were apparent as far back as the early 2000s from confessions and parent concerns, but the typical bureaucratic delayed responses and obfuscations enabled Krivinov's criminal momentum to grow basically unchecked.

While ultimately defrocked and convicted on abuse and animal cruelty charges, Krivinov's 12 year sentence left many outraged over perceived leniency. A mistrust of church motivations to downplay the scope remains palpable in Rudnevo today.

Alwy M. Jones

Orthodox Church Krasnodar Krai, Russia

Father Gerasim Gogin, a 37 year old priest serving at the Church of All Saints in the village of Kazhidonskaya, now faces charges for the sexual assault of two young boys in separate incidents, along with criminal threats and obstructing justice.

The first victim, a 10 year old boy from Kazhidonskaya, was lured by the priest under the pretense of "an errand" as Gogin drove him to a remote forest location. There, according to court documents, the priest threatened the boy saying he must obey and submit to Gogin without argument, referencing God's will that demands his obedience to a man of God.

Gogin then raped the young boy through vile, degrading acts of sexual violence and domination, according to the shocking charges of molesting and soiling this child's innocence. Afterwards, he issued an overt threat to murder the boy if he ever revealed what happened, thus instilling fear and domination over the child.

This child abuse and sacrilege compounded by the priest's attempts to use his authority as a man of God to force submission directly contravening the pure, light, and grace that should define God's service has rocked the rural congregation and devout community.

The sordid affair deepened when the priest's second sick crime came to light; approaching an 8 year old boy and deceiving him with the same manipulative tactics, forcing a horrific encounter with immoral dominance and psychological trauma.

For the close knit, God fearing community of Kazhidozkaya to have a spiritual leader committing such depraved, unholy crimes against young boys tore at the sanctity of their faith, stripping them of dignity and light in direct service to the dark, evil and shame.

Reverend Gogin exploited his spiritual rank and divine calling, using his holy robes not as a garb of honor and light, but as a despicable wolf's cloak of immorality concealing his vile acts of child rape and fear instilling dominance.

Christianity in Africa

In the newscast of S2 Aktuell, Germany, a station not at all critical to Christianity, the following was stated:

Anglican as well as Catholic priests and nuns are suspect of having actively participated in murders. Especially the conduct of a certain Catholic priest has been occupying the public mind in Rwanda's capital Kigali for months. He was minister of the church of the Holy Family and allegedly murdered Tutsis in the most brutal manner. He is reported to have accompanied marauding Hutu militia with a gun in his cowl. In fact there has been a bloody slaughter of Tutsis seeking shelter in his parish. Even two years after the massacres many Catholics refuse to set foot on the threshold of their church, because to them the participation of a certain part of the clergy in the slaughter is well established. There is almost no church in Rwanda that has not seen refugees; women, children, old being brutally butchered facing the crucifix.

According to eyewitnesses clergymen gave away hiding Tutsis and turned them over to the machetes of the Hutu militia.

In connection with these events two Benedictine nuns are mentioned, both of whom have fled into a Belgian monastery in the meantime to avoid prosecution. According to survivors one of them called the Hutu killers and led them to several thousand people who had sought shelter in her monastery. By force the doomed were driven out of the churchyard and were murdered in the presence of the nun right in front of the gate. The other one is also reported to have directly cooperated with the murderers of the Hutu militia. In her case again witnesses report that she watched the slaughtering of people in cold blood and without showing response. She is even accused of having procured some petrol used by the killers to set on fire and burn their victims alive…

As can be seen from these events, to Christianity the Dark Ages never come to an end….

The Case of Juan Severino Mallari

Juan Severino Mallari, a Catholic priest born in 1765, allegedly used his position of spiritual authority to commit a string of grisly murders over a span of several decades beginning in the 1780s. Contemporary accounts describe him as an intense, severe man who struck a frightening presence.

The earliest recorded victims were young altar boys from churches where Mallari was stationed in rural provinces. However, the pool of presumed targets expanded over time to include female parishioners, traveling friars, Indigenous folk who wandered too near Mallari's churches, and any others who angered or disappointed him.

Supposed motives for his pathological criminality ranged from sadistic sexual perversions to religiously motivated sacrificial rituals carried out with an almost inquisitorial zeal. Some accused Mallari of pagan deviations and witchcraft, seeing occult significance in the symbolic mutilations of bodies.

Whenever a rash of disappearances or body discoveries around one of his postings grew too flagrant, Spanish authorities would simply reassign Mallari, allowing him to sew terror in a new community. The far-flung nature of the rural parishes made communication and coordination difficult.

Mallari's luck ran out in 1839 when a young postulant personally witnessed him brutalize and slay an elderly Chinese immigrant near the church grounds. Though the postulant's frantic report was initially dismissed, further outrage and scrutiny revealed a homicidal career spanning 55 years and potentially upwards of 50-60 unfortunate souls met with Mallari's barbaric brand of ritual judgment.

Authorities finally arrested Mallari, who by this time had adopted a raving persona and alternated between vehement claims of innocence and boasts of conversing with dark spirits. Placed on trial in Manila in 1840, he was swiftly convicted and garroted publicly in an infamous execution where he reportedly cursed and spat at onlookers until the end.

In the aftermath, the case exposed the unchecked autonomy of malign parish priests in the colonial era and the systemic failure to monitor accusations against moral authorities like Mallari. Many Filipino families learned of innocent loved ones who had fallen victim to his bloodlust, compounding the generational trauma.

Central African Republic Ripped Apart by Anti-Balaka Reign of Terror

What began as a grassroots Christian movement has mutated into a devastating campaign of ethnic cleansing and secular violence, threatening to tear apart the Central African Republic.

In the wake of the 2013 overthrow of President Francois Bozize by the Seleka rebel alliance, the anti-balaka militia emerged to counter the rebel coalition. However, their actions have descended into an organized crusade to purge Muslim communities from swaths of the country through indiscriminate killing, rape, and the torching of entire villages. They attacked at dawn, shouting anti-Muslim slurs, they burned down homes and the mosque.

Scene after scene of charred homes, belongings, and houses of worship bear witness to the anti-balaka's brutality unleashed upon Muslim enclaves. Interviews with survivors paint a portrait of summary executions, women and girls abducted and raped, and entire families forced to seek refuge hundreds of miles away.

A growing trend of disenfranchised youth being radicalized and recruited by hardline anti-balaka commanders often with financial incentives. Some of these young militants were former church altar boys, others are drawn by the promise of cash earned from manning roadside checkpoints that extort money from Muslims desperate to flee.

Capitalizing on longstanding religious divisions and economic despair in the embattled nation, anti-balaka leaders seemingly allowed the worst impulses and prejudices of angry, armed young men to take over.

Unconfirmed reports also suggest links between the anti-balaka militias and wealthy Christian businessmen covertly bankrolling the violence. Their rumored endgame? Permanently redrawing the demographics by eliminating Muslim populations from Christian majority areas.

In the capital of Bangui alone, over 500 Muslims were killed since December and nearly the entire community evacuated from the flashpoint PK5 neighborhood after a spate of anti-balaka raids and massacres at mosques.

Countrywide, over 600,000 remain internally displaced from the anti-balaka threat, living in squalid camps and hiding in the bush with little access to food, water or basic services. An estimated 290,000 Muslims; over half the pre-crisis population have fled across borders into Chad, Cameroon and beyond.

The heavy toll of civilian suffering lays bare the grim reality of the anti-balaka's endgame using terror tactics and sheer brutality to erase the country's Muslim communities through death or displacement.

The Manili Massacre

It was supposed to be a peaceful gathering to rally support for an upcoming election. But the events of June 24th 1971 in the coastal town of Manili would instead become seared into history as one of the Philippines' darkest and most brutal episodes of violence.

That morning, over 1,500 Moro Muslim men, women and children converged at the town plaza to support the gubernatorial candidacy of Rashid Lucman. Political tensions were already running high on Mindanao between Muslim minority groups like the Moros and Christian majorities jockeying for power.

According to eyewitness accounts, military forces under the command of the province's Christian governor opened fire indiscriminately as the political rally was just getting started. Lucman and his running mate were killed in the initial barrage. But the massacre was just beginning.

The soldiers showed no mercy, spraying bullets into the panicked crowd, bodies were piling everywhere, children screaming while clinging to their dead parents.

Over the course of several hours, the soldiers methodically slaughtered hundreds of Moro victims in a horrific killing spree. No one was spared, the elderly, women and children, even local Muslims coming to aid the wounded. First-hand accounts describe bodies being bayoneted and assaulted with barbaric cruelty.

When the dust settled, as many as 80 Moro Muslims are estimated to have perished, one of the worst single atrocities of modern Philippines history. Some remains were buried in mass graves while shattered families carted away other corpses in trucks, oxcarts and even woven banana leaves.

In the ensuing decades, the Manili massacre has attained historical infamy as a prime catalyst for the escalating Moro separatist conflict. It inspired a generation of Moro fighters joining the Moro National Liberation Front.

Alwy M. Jones

Moro Muslims Still Haunted by Another Massacre

On that fateful day, Muslim Moro villagers were preparing to celebrate the Islamic holiday of Eid al-Fitr, marking the end of Ramadan. But the festivities were shattered amid the volleys of gunfire and mortar shells that rained down on the farming community without warning.

For the next several hours, elements of the Philippine Constabulary; the precursor to the national police along with paramilitary fighters engaged in a systematic slaughter of men, women and children simply due to their Moro ethnicity and faith.

When the dust settled, Tacub lay in carnage and ruin. Estimates of the death toll at least 300. Rotting bodies littered the roads and clogged irrigation canals. Dozens of survivors bore horrific injuries like severed limbs and gunshot wounds.

At the center of the bloodshed was a single family's home, where the floors and walls were found caked in the grisly evidence of children executed at point-blank range and women sexually assaulted before their deaths. It revealed the massacre's unspeakable brutality.

Four decades later, the trauma endures like an open wound within Tacub and the wider Moro community on the island of Mindanao. The Philippine government initially denied the atrocities, calling it a defensive assault on Moro secessionists. It was not until the Ramos administration in 1995 that the state acknowledged its culpability.

Today, a modest monument stands in Tacub commemorating the lives lost. It remains an annual pilgrimage site for relatives seeking to honor the massacre's countless victims. But justice and accountability remain frustratingly elusive for many.

The Moro Massacre and the First Battle of Bud Dajo

The Moro Massacre, also known as the First Battle of Bud Dajo, took place from March 5-7, 1906, on the island of Jolo in the southern Philippines. This conflict pitted American colonial forces against the Moro people, the Muslim inhabitants of the region who had fiercely resisted Spanish rule for centuries and were now facing a new foreign power.

The battle centered around Bud Dajo, a dormant volcanic crater where approximately 800-1,000 Moro villagers, including women and children, had taken refuge. They were resisting the American colonial administration's attempts to impose taxes and disarm the population. The American forces, led by Major General Leonard Wood, deployed a force of about 790 men, including Army and Navy personnel. They were armed with modern weapons, including artillery and machine guns.

The ensuing battle was extremely one sided. Despite the Moros' determined resistance, they were armed primarily with traditional weapons like kris swords and spears, with only a few firearms. The American forces' superior firepower, including the use of artillery, resulted in devastating casualties among the Moro defenders.

Official reports indicate that 600 to 900 Moros were killed, including many women and children. In contrast, American casualties were minimal, with 21 killed and 73 wounded. The disproportionate nature of the casualties and the inclusion of non-combatants among the dead led to significant controversy. The significance of this event cannot be overstated. For the Moro people, it represented a brutal assertion of American colonial power and a tragic loss of life. It deepened the distrust between the Moros and their new colonial rulers, setting the stage for continued resistance.

In the broader historical context, the Bud Dajo massacre occurred during a period of American expansionism and the height of the colonial era. It highlighted the ethical dilemmas and contradictions inherent in the American colonial project, which espoused ideals of freedom and democracy while engaging in acts of violence against indigenous populations.

The impact on the Muslim community was profound and long lasting. The massacre became a rallying point for Moro resistance and a key element in their historical narrative. It reinforced their sense of distinct identity and their determination to preserve their culture and autonomy.

The events at Bud Dajo also foreshadowed the complex relationship between the Philippine central government and the Moro people that persists to this day. The struggle for autonomy and recognition of Moro rights has been a recurring theme in Philippine politics, with echoes of the resistance that led to the Bud Dajo massacre.

- After the Battle at Mount Dajo on Jolo island, Sulu province. March 7, 1906. US military under the command of Major General Leonard Wood bombed the stronghold killing over 600 men, women and children.

Palimbang's Wounds Still Unhealed

It was the early morning of June 28th 1986 when nearly 1,000 members of the civilian forces of the Ilaga, a Christian militia group surrounded and laid siege to Palimbang. At the time, this small rural community with a population around 1,500 was home to ethnic Moro Muslim farmers and their families.

What unfolded over the next two days was nothing short of a systematic and brutal massacre. Armed only with farming tools and antiquated firearms, the outnumbered Moro residents were helpless against the Ilaga forces' military grade weapons and brutal onslaught.

By June 29th, over 350 bodies of Moro Muslims had been pulled from torched homes and killing fields around Palimbang, according to government tallies. Hundreds more wounded fled into the surrounding jungle. Later investigations found many of the dead had been sexually assaulted, dismembered and mutilated in grotesque displays of savagery.

For Palimbang's few surviving Moro residents, the massacre obliterated their community in the span of 48 hours, displacing almost the entire population into nearby refugee camps. Loved ones' remains were hastily buried in mass graves by the Philippine military in subsequent days.

The massacre's extreme brutality fueled outrage across the Muslim world and tarnished international perceptions of the Philippines' human rights record.

It strengthened the resolve of armed Moro factions like the MILF.

Most crucially, Palimbang underscored the dangers of using civilian paramilitary or militia forces against minority populations, with the potential for unrestrained violence and civilian casualties. Subsequent governments disavowed ties with such groups.

Today, Palimbang is a largely empty husk amid the lingering air of despondency. A few dozen former residents were the only ones willing to return post-massacre.

Alwy M. Jones

Kattankudy's Wounds of Hatred Still Unhealed

The evening call to prayer had just echoed through this Muslim majority town on August 3rd1990, when the peace was shattered by the staccato cracks of gunfire and explosions. A band of heavily armed militants had surrounded the Meera Hussain Jumma Mosque and were slaughtering worshippers indiscriminately as they emerged.

By that night's end, at least 147 Muslim civilians; men, women and children as young as 14 months old lay dead in pools of blood. Scores more were wounded, some losing limbs from the grenades lobbed into the packed mosque. It ranked among the worst single massacres of the Sri Lankan civil war's bloody history.

Over three decades later, the motive behind why this house of worship was so savagely targeted remains hotly disputed. But the scars it inflicted endure as a haunting open wound for Kattankudy's Muslim community.

While an official government probe initially charged the attack as ethnic cleansing carried out by the Liberation Tigers of Tamil Eelam (LTTE) separatist group, the LTTE has steadfastly denied responsibility. Some reports instead accuse a breakaway Tamil militant faction working with anti-Muslim Sinhalese accomplices of orchestrating the slaughter, possibly to stoke further ethnic tensions between minority groups.

Alwy M. Jones

For Sri Lanka's Muslim population, estimated around 2 million at the time, the Kattankudy massacre represented an alarming escalation of separatist violence targeting their community after largely being bystanders in the Tamil-Sinhalese civil conflict. In the subsequent months and years, reports of Muslims being forcibly expelled from Tamil controlled areas spiked.

Today the blood stained Mosque has been repaired and refurbished, its walls repainted but not free of lingering haunting reminders. An annual vigil is still held outside its walls to commemorate the lives senselessly extinguished. But issues around accountability and memorializing the victims remain fraught with controversy.

Some Tamil minority leaders have sought to diminish or ignore the Kattankudy atrocities completely, fearing it could detract from their narrative of persecution by the Sinhalese-led Sri Lankan government forces during the civil war. The government, meanwhile, has done little to push any deeper investigations over fears of triggering renewed ethnic distrust.

The result, say mosque trustees, leaves an open wound of trauma inflicted by extremist forces that has never healed what should amount to a searing crime against humanity not fully recognized in the war's aftermath.

Alwy M. Jones

The Reinvention of Christ: Da Vinci's Controversial Commission for the Borgias

In the dawning years of the 16th century Renaissance, the ruling dynasty of Pope Alexander VI held authoritarian grip over the Papal States and Vatican City. But the house of Borgia also wielded an underrated influence over Christianity's very cultural and artistic canon.

It was during this turbulent era in 1506 that Cesare Borgia, the powerful and ruthless son of the Pope, summoned the young Leonardo da Vinci to his court. The commission he presented the Tuscan genius seems, at first glance, incongruous to render an unconventional portrait depicting Jesus Christ as a white European renaissance man.

It was an encapsulation of how the Borgias used faith as a velvet glove to mask their corruption and consolidate power. Their humanist scholars promoted this revision of Christ's traditional imagery purely out of vainglory.

For centuries prior, iconic representations of the Christian Savior preserved His Middle Eastern Semitic appearance; olive skin, dark features and callused hands reflecting his humble carpenter roots. But under the patronage of Cesare Borgia and Pope Alexander, a movement took hold within the Church to "Europeanize" Christ's visage into a canonical paradigm of masculine, Aryan perfection.

Art experts note Cesare specifically instructed da Vinci to portray Christ with the idealized, elongated proportions and swept back light hair of High Renaissance sculpture. The end result is a strikingly divergent, almost profane departure from centuries of traditional Christian iconography.

While da Vinci's painting has been lost to history, contemporaries described the portrait as "of a noble, serene and gentle nature, yet fully a semblance of the divine." But the mere notion was deemed highly controversial, both within the Church as well as by secular dissidents critical of the Borgia family's corruption and excesses.

Some speculate whether Cesare's motivations were more calculated, an attempt to weaponize the symbolism of a de-ethicized Christ figure among the malleable Catholic masses to augment his own claims of dynastic divinity and authority over spirituality itself. As the Vatican's de facto warlord and privateer, such ambitions would align with the Borgia's unchecked hedonism and overreach.

Other scholars counter that Cesare's aims were more in line with perpetuating a whitewashing trend of Eurocentrism already embedded within Renaissance artistic culture. By commissioning the art world's sharpest luminary in Da Vinci to advance a classic Caucasian aesthetic, the Church was sanctifying and codifying bigoted notions of European racial supremacy as central to the iconography of their faith.

Alwy M. Jones

Si Ali Sakkat's Lifesaving Defiance

On the outskirts of Tunis in 1942, as the horrors of the Holocaust encroached across North Africa, an unlikely Muslim factory worker put his life on the line to shelter persecuted Jews fleeing the occupying Nazi forces and their collaborators.

His name was Si Ali Sakkat, and over a span of two years, he provided sanctuary and safe passage for nearly two dozen Jewish families and individuals in the face of grave personal jeopardy.

Sakkat's bravery stemmed from a deeply moral conviction, upheld not just by himself but many in the Muslim neighborhoods of La Goulette. A cobbler by trade, he and his wife Medina opened their humble home near the Jewish quarters to shield people from the Nazi's genocidal dragnet after hearing the gut wrenching testimonies of early escapees.

Despite edicts and propaganda from Nazi commanders calling for the extermination of the Jews, the Sakkats were emblematic of the relative tolerance and acceptance Jews had historically experienced among Muslim communities in North Africa compared to Christian persecution in Europe.

Si Ali believed it was simply the right thing to do, Jews were fellow human beings living among them for centuries. When the Nazis came with their evil to destroy that, he saw it as a moral and spiritual duty to resist such hatred.

But the risks of such resistance cannot be overstated. Under the iron boot of occupation, even the slightest hints of defiance or dissent invited the most draconian reprisals from the Nazis and their henchmen. Some took courage from rare moments like the famed Tunisian Revolt of 1942, which resulted in hundreds of civilian deaths.

Sakkat himself surely witnessed the aftermath of such brutality when Nazis looted the city's ancient Jewish Quarter and rounded up nearly 5000 Jews for deportation to forced labor camps that year. Smuggling refugees through those tightened strangleholds necessitated a constant haze of secrecy, constantly shifting safe houses, and placing unwavering trust in strangers.

After Tunisia's liberation in 1943, Sakkat's humanitarianism came to light. He played a vital role getting Jewish refugees to safe havens like Djerba Island or preparing exodus boats to carry evacuees toward British held Palestine. Some estimates suggest he helped at least 24 Jewish families around 100 individuals evade unthinkable fates at the hands of the Nazis.

Alwy M. Jones

How Ireland's Tragedy Shaped an Ottoman Sultan's Stance

In June 1847, while the devastating potato blight that spawned the Great Hunger in Ireland reached its peak over a thousand miles away, its ripples extended even to the court of the Ottoman Sultan Abdul Majid I. Contemporary accounts suggest the young caliph followed the reports of mass starvation and emigration with increasing outrage.

The torture of Erin by the English is a defilement of the world in the eyes of God," Sultan Majid proclaimed in an address to his council. He was particularly incensed by the British policies that, by many accounts, exacerbated the famine's death toll through prioritizing commodity exports over delivering food aid.

While no official protest was lodged by the Sublime Porte, British ambassadors reported heated rhetoric from high ranking Ottoman officials decrying the "cruel neglect" of the Irish people. Sultan Majid privately indicated support for Irish nationalist ambitions, having already butted heads with London over territorial conflicts in Aden and Greek independence.

Some historians believe the Famine colored Majid's increasingly anti-British reputation in his later years. In 1853, he would back the Russian alliance against Britain and France in the Crimean War, though the young reformer's motivations were also driven by his hopes to modernize and defend the fraying Ottoman frontiers.

For the destitute, famine afflicted Irish masses, the Sultan's condemnations and diplomatic jockeying did little to ease their suffering directly. But his impassioned statements reflected how the unprecedented crisis in Ireland reverberated around the world and among even the most powerful Muslim sovereigns of the day.

The Sultan Majid offered 10,000 British pounds which has a current value of over 1.3 million USD.

Mossad's Clandestine Footprints in South Africa Uncovered

For decades, the extent of Israel's intelligence agency Mossad's operations on South African soil largely remained an open secret; spies of the shadows with plausible deniability. However, recent events and whistleblower accounts have shed disturbing light on the scope and audacity of these covert activities, hinting at a foreign interference campaign that could fundamentally impact the nation's security and sovereignty.

According to insider sources and investigations by South African media, the Mossad's presence is suspected of encompassing;

- Intelligence gathering on South Africa's nuclear program and materials

- Economic espionage and theft of defense/technology secrets

- Supporting and arming anti-ANC guerilla groups during Apartheid era

- Tracking South Africa's relations and dealings with Iran and other rivals

- Aggressive recruitment of South African citizens as informant assets

Unsurprisingly, South African officials have reacted to these disclosures with outrage over the violation of national sovereignty but also admissions that widespread Mossad actions were long suspected if not confirmed.

In late 2019, President Cyril Ramaphosa's office officially designated the Mossad a "hostile impending force" following reports of rogue operatives attempting to bribe top officials for assistance monitoring Iranian assets.

Pretoria has also protested what it calls Israel's "weaponising" of South Africa's 50,000 strong Jewish community as a pool of potential moles a highly sensitive accusation given the apartheid regime's history of discrimination.

At least nine South Africans have been arrested under the country's anti-terror and secrecy laws since 2015 for alleged collaboration with the Mossad, among them senior intelligence operatives in the SSA agency.

South Africa's tangled ties with Israel and Iran further blur the ethical lines for Mossad conduct. Pretoria has developed warm relations with Tehran, a sworn enemy of the Jewish state.

Alwy M. Jones

Uncovering the Unsettling Global Footprint of Israel's Election Meddlers

When Canadian investigative researchers exposed the shadowy Israeli firm Emerdata's apparent attempts to discreetly malign and sabotage political figures during Alberta's 2022 provincial election, it laid bare what experts describe as merely the tip of a disquieting iceberg of foreign interference.

Emerdata's digital footprints has been mapped to over 30 elections across five continents just in the last decade, along with other notorious private intelligence firms that appear to leverage Israeli intelligence assets and cyber operatives. The reality? A sprawling, lucrative private industry of electoral manipulation services all too easily attainable globally.

Based in Occupied Palestinian Territories and founded by former Israeli intelligence operatives, companies like Emerdata, Black Cube, Terragence and their ilk effectively privatized the "black bag" tactics of traditional state espionage. Their array of services pedaled? Disinformation dissemination, persona impersonation, viral amplification through troll farms, and hacking of politicians and their advisors.

These groups don't just dabble in cyber offensives, they offer comprehensive election interference packages, everything from honey trap stings to deep fake video distribution against a target. All conveniently outsourced.

One Canadian client reported paying Emerdata over $80,000 to promote fake scandals and proliferation of inflammatory hashtags targeting their political foes. In Michigan's 2022 gubernatorial race, Terragence employees were caught impersonating student activists hurling anti-Palestinian smears at the Democratic candidate.

Investigation identified Emerdata's cyber fingerprints on at least 35 elections globally since 2014, spanning contests in Malaysia, Germany, South Africa, Brazil, and the United Arab Emirates. Evidence points to the firm's potential disruptions in nine additional contests as well.

The tentacles appear even more widespread for an outfit like Black Cube, founded by former Israeli intelligence officers. This group, exposed for its attempted stings on Obama staffers, has been linked to election info-ops in over a dozen African nations alone according to leaked archives.

They market themselves as the next generation of private geopolitical risk managing firms, but when your recruitment pipeline is sourced directly from former Mossad cyber divisions, there's a glaring conflict of interest regarding how these capabilities are being unleashed.

All of these firms have denied any involvement in improper electoral misconduct. An Emerdata statement claimed its activities are simply "civic engagement services" intended to "strengthen democracy." Black Cube has dismissed all allegations of impropriety as "rank misinformation."

The motivations behind such mercenary campaigns seemed largely financial, ideological and geopolitical in nature. Emerdata operatives are believed to harbor strong Zionist sympathies and have been contracted by clients sympathetic to right wing settler movements.

Black Cube and other Israeli based groups cultivate close ties to oligarch and pro-Israel donors who can access their disruptive services. But the biggest customer is quite clearly authoritarians and illiberal interests looking to cling to power and undermine democratic institutions, pointing to the firm's presence across nations like Zimbabwe, Republic of Congo and Cambodia.

The implications for sovereign democratic processes, and the precedent of open for hire foreign interference are nothing short of chilling for those elevating ethics over profits.

Perhaps most alarmingly, analysts broadly believe the public scratches visible are only fractionally revealing the true extent of these firms' covert activities in privatizing election meddling at a global scale.

Alwy M. Jones

Mossad's Femme Fatales and the Dark Arts of Honey trapping

In the cloak and dagger tradecraft of international espionage, few tactics have retained as much mystique and psychological potency as the concept of "honey trapping"; deploying attractive agents in weaponized seduction to beguile targets into revealing sensitive information or compromising access. And few agencies have cultivated as fearsome a reputation for masterfully wielding these lethally charming "femme fatales" as Israel's renowned Mossad intelligence service.

Honey trapping's very moniker conjures up equal parts intrigue and discomfort - referencing the insect snaring and life-draining attributes of its namesake. At its core, the tactic preys on the most primal of human frailties; lust, ego, and the irresistible temptation of forbidden indulgence dangled by a beguiling source.

Former CIA case officer Lindsay Moran doesn't mince words: "It's a cold, highly manipulative act, something straight out of a Robert Ludlum novel except very real. You're simply using your body to obtain information that could potentially endanger lives and security."

Yet honey traps have arguably represented one of the most potent psychological operations platforms throughout intelligence communities. A well-executed operation can extract everything from state secrets to cyber passwords to biometric identities, all through the sheer gravitational pull of seductive leverage by an operative strategically embodying the target's suppressed desires.

And in a #MeToo era of evolving gender dynamics, honey trapping has also witnessed a curious role reversal with male assets now equally deployed as "honey badgers" to similarly exploit female target vulnerabilities. While biology may give the edge to feminine fatales as more effective lures, toxic masculinity's pitfalls appear an equal opportunity employer.

If any agency has mastered the darkly salacious arts of honey trapping to the level of tradecraft science, it's the Mossad, the virtuosos of Israel's vaunted intelligence arsenal. According to insider accounts and defectors, their training techniques in sexual entrapment are intensive and clinical, nurturing attractive young recruits into expert manipulators skilled at adopting tailor made personas to disarm designated targets.

This is, of course, a world of open secrets. While Israeli officials steadfastly deny the very existence of what's euphemistically termed a "Honey Trap" division, their honey trapping prowess has been an open source of infamy and awe.

The Mossad's women recruits are trained in seduction maneuvers the same way their male counterparts learn small arms," whistleblower Victor Ostrovsky, a former Mossad katsa officer, revealed decades ago.

"Sex instruction utilizing psychology and interpreting body signals."

While sensationalized Hollywood depictions may verge on misogynistic fantasy, the Mossad's real world honey trapping operations have run the gamut, from assassinations of foes to capturing adversaries.

In 1986, a Mossad femme fatale managed to lure her mark; a senior Syrian intelligence officer to rendezvous points by portraying herself as a beguiling Mexican mistress, only for him to be drugged and repatriated to Israel. Intelligence motherlodes don't come richer than a high level Arab intelligence asset captured through unadulterated carnal guile.

Of darker infamy was the 2010 Dubai sting, where a team of Mossad agents including several women operatives in supporting roles assassinated Hamas operative Mahmoud al-Mabhouh in his hotel room after trailing him on multiple romanticized honey trap rendezvous dates.

No evidence ever surfaced that Mabhouh was physically seduced on those final fateful encounters. But the mere omnipresence of potential honey trapping intrigue paralyzed the Palestinian's usual operational vigilance.

Alwy M. Jones

Regarding The 1994 Israeli Embassy Bombing in London

According to Anne Machon, who resigned from MI5 in 1997 to blow the whistle on alleged improprieties, there was credible intelligence that Mossad, the Israeli intelligence agency, had actually orchestrated the bombing of its own embassy in the British capital. Her claims first surfaced in the late 1990s and resurfaced over the years.

The official narrative was that the bombing was carried out by Palestinian militants in retaliation for the killing of their leaders by Israel. However, Machon alleges that MI5 had monitored Israeli embassy communications that indicated Mossad was going to carry out a "false flag" attack and then blame it on Palestinian groups.

What's Machon's potential evidence? Primarily intelligence communications intercepted by MI5 pointing to Israeli foreknowledge, which she says was inexplicably ignored by her superiors. She has also claimed there were Mossad agents present in London around that time under homeland security coverage.

This means one of America's closest allies in the Middle East had conducted a bombing on British soil that killed over 20 people, for purposes still unclear. It could have significantly strained the UK's relations with Israel diplomatically, economically and in intelligence sharing.

However, Machon's allegations have been vehemently denied by Israeli officials. British government inquiries found no evidence of her claims. MI5 has responded that Machon's credibility is compromised after breaking secrecy codes herself. Some observers argue foreign agencies cannot always fully investigate such explosive claims for sake of diplomacy.

Ultimately, the 1994 Israeli embassy bombing remains an officially unsolved case. Without more concrete evidence surfacing, Anne Machon's allegations are unlikely to drastically rewrite the historical understanding, but the controversy lingers. As is often the case in intelligence scandals, the truth remains obscured by clouds of secrecy, political convenience and combating narratives. The implications of Machon's claims remind us that even ally nations guard their own interests above all else in the shadowy world of espionage.

Alwy M. Jones

Jews and the Trans-Atlantic Slave Trade

The story of the slave ship "Four Sisters" operated by Jewish merchant Moses Levy sheds light on an often overlooked aspect of the transatlantic slave trade; the involvement of Jewish merchants, traders, and ship owners.

In the late 18th century, Moses Levy, a Jewish merchant from Newport, Rhode Island, was one of the most prominent traders and ship owners involved in the transatlantic slave trade. His infamous ship, the "Four Sisters," made numerous voyages between the coast of West Africa and the Caribbean, transporting thousands of enslaved Africans across the Middle Passage.

Jewish participation in the slave trade was not unique to Levy or Newport. Historical records indicate that Jewish merchants, financiers, and ship owners were involved in the slave trade in various capacities across the Americas, Europe, and the Caribbean. Some played pivotal roles in facilitating the transportation, sale, and exploitation of enslaved Africans, driven by the pursuit of economic gain and integration into the broader mercantile systems of the time.

The involvement of Jewish individuals and communities in the slave trade has often been downplayed or overlooked in historical narratives, partly due to the sensitivity surrounding the topic and the desire to separate the Jewish experience from the atrocities of slavery. However, confronting this aspect of history is crucial to gaining a comprehensive understanding of the transatlantic slave trade and it's far reaching consequences.

The story of the "Four Sisters" and Moses Levy's role in the slave trade raises important questions about the intersections of religion, economics, and human exploitation. It challenges the notion that participation in the slave trade was solely a matter of racial or ethnic dynamics, and instead highlights the complex interplay of economic incentives, cultural assimilation, and the normalization of dehumanizing practices.

Anne & Eliza' by Justus Bosch and John Abrams

The painting, completed in 2023, depicts two young African women, Anne and Eliza, who were enslaved and owned by the Jewish merchant Abraham Rodrigues Mendes in colonial New York in the late 17th century. The artwork has garnered significant attention for its unflinching representation of the involvement of Jewish individuals in the slave trade, a topic that has often been overlooked or obscured in historical narratives.

Historical records indicate that Jewish individuals and communities were involved in various aspects of the slave trade, from financing and facilitating the transportation of enslaved Africans to owning and trading enslaved people themselves. In colonial New York, where the painting's subjects lived, Jewish merchants like Abraham Rodrigues Mendes played a significant role in the city's slave owning economy.

Some examples are Jewish settlers in Dutch Brazil, Caribbean islanders like the Jew's of Curacao, and certain merchants in cities like Newport, Charleston and Savannah.

Pfizer in Nigeria during the 1990s.

In 1996, during a devastating meningitis epidemic in Kano, Nigeria, Pfizer conducted clinical trials for its experimental antibiotic drug, Trovan (trovafloxacin). The trials involved 200 children, who were recruited from a crowded infectious disease hospital. Half of the children received Trovan, while the other half received a comparator drug, Ceftriaxone, which was already approved for treating meningitis in children.

In 2001, a group of Nigerian families filed a lawsuit against Pfizer, alleging that the company had conducted unethical and illegal drug trials on their children without proper consent or adequate safety monitoring. The plaintiffs claimed that Pfizer had failed to obtain informed consent from the children's parents or legal guardians, and that the trials had caused serious injuries and deaths.

Pfizer denied the allegations, arguing that the trials were conducted in accordance with international ethical standards and Nigerian laws. The company claimed that it had obtained appropriate approvals from the Nigerian government and that the trials were necessary to test the effectiveness of Trovan in treating meningitis during the epidemic.

The case, Abdullahi v. Pfizer, Inc., was filed in a federal court in New York. After years of legal battles, the case went to trial in 2009. During the trial, evidence was presented that raised serious concerns about Pfizer's conduct, including allegations of forged consent forms, inadequate monitoring of the participants, and a failure to provide proper medical care.

In 2009, after a lengthy trial, the case was settled out of court for $75 million, which was to be distributed among the families of the affected children. The settlement also included provisions for the establishment of a healthcare facility in Kano to treat neurological disorders, which were allegedly caused by the experimental drug.

The Abdullahi v. Pfizer, Inc. case raised significant ethical concerns about the conduct of clinical trials, particularly in developing countries where vulnerable populations may be at risk of exploitation. The case highlighted the need for stricter regulations and oversight to ensure that pharmaceutical companies adhere to ethical standards and prioritize the safety and well-being of trial participants.

Critics argued that Pfizer's actions demonstrated a lack of respect for human dignity and autonomy, as well as a disregard for the principles of informed consent and ethical research practices. The case also raised questions about the role of Western pharmaceutical companies in developing countries and the potential for exploiting vulnerable populations for financial gain.

Alwy M. Jones

The AZT Trials and Ethical Concerns

In the late 1990s, researchers from the United States conducted clinical trials in several African countries, including Zimbabwe, to test the efficacy of a shorter course of the antiretroviral drug AZT (zidovudine) in preventing mother to child transmission of HIV. These trials were sponsored by the National Institutes of Health (NIH) and the Centers for Disease Control and Prevention (CDC).

The trials involved pregnant women with HIV who were randomly assigned to receive either a short course of AZT or a placebo. At the time, a longer course of AZT was already the standard treatment in the United States and other developed countries for preventing mother to child transmission of HIV.

The ethical concerns surrounding these trials centered on the fact that the researchers knowingly withheld the proven, longer course of AZT treatment from the placebo group, effectively denying them the established standard of care. Critics argued that this violated fundamental ethical principles, such as beneficence (the obligation to maximize benefits and minimize harm) and respect for persons (the recognition of individuals' autonomy and right to make informed decisions).

One of the most controversial trials took place in Zimbabwe, where researchers from the University of Zimbabwe, in collaboration with Johns Hopkins University and the CDC, conducted a study on HIV positive pregnant women. The study aimed to compare the efficacy of a shorter course of AZT with a placebo in preventing mother to child transmission of HIV.

According to reports, the trial involved over 17,000 HIV positive pregnant women, and the placebo group consisted of approximately 1,000 participants. Shockingly, despite the availability of the proven, longer course of AZT treatment, the researchers chose not to provide it to the placebo group, resulting in the transmission of HIV to approximately 1,000 babies.

This decision sparked outrage and condemnation from bioethicists, human rights organizations, and the international community. Critics argued that the researchers had violated ethical principles by knowingly exposing infants to the risk of contracting HIV when an effective preventive treatment was readily available.

The AZT trials in Africa, particularly the Zimbabwe study, ignited a fierce debate about the ethics of conducting clinical trials in developing countries, where access to standard treatments may be limited. The case highlighted the potential for exploitation of vulnerable populations and the need for stronger ethical oversight and regulations.

In response to the controversy, the United States government and international organizations issued guidelines and regulations aimed at ensuring that clinical trials involving human subjects in developing countries adhere to ethical principles and provide access to established, effective treatments.

Additionally, the case prompted calls for greater community engagement, informed consent processes, and the involvement of local ethics review boards in clinical trials conducted in developing countries. It also emphasized the importance of ensuring that research benefits not only the sponsors but also the communities where the trials are conducted.

Alwy M. Jones

Forced sexual reassignment in South Africa

The forced sexual reassignment surgeries carried out by Dr. Aubrey Levin on South African soldiers during the apartheid era in the 1970s and 1980s were a grave violation of human rights and medical ethics. This disturbing practice, which targeted young men who were perceived as potentially gay or "gender non-conforming," has been described as one of the most egregious examples of state sanctioned conversion therapy and abusive military policies.

Dr. Aubrey Levin was a military psychiatrist and the head of the male circumcision clinic at Voortrekkerhoogte Military Hospital in Pretoria, South Africa. During the apartheid regime's conscription of white males into the military, Levin was tasked with identifying and "curing" homosexual or effeminate draftees.

Under the guise of medical treatment, Levin subjected numerous young soldiers to unethical and inhumane practices, including forced sex change operations. These procedures, which were performed without proper consent or regard for the individuals' well-being, involved the surgical removal of testicles and the construction of artificial vaginas.

Levin's rationale for these surgeries was rooted in the belief that homosexuality was a mental disorder that could be "cured" through radical medical interventions. He claimed that the surgeries would "alter" the individuals' sexual orientation and make them more masculine, aligning with the military's heteronormative ideals.

The forced sexual reassignment surgeries perpetrated by Levin and sanctioned by the apartheid military establishment constituted a gross violation of human rights and medical ethics. These practices violated fundamental principles of autonomy, informed consent, and the do no harm principle that guides medical practice.

Many victims reported experiencing severe physical and psychological trauma as a result of the surgeries, which were often performed without their knowledge or understanding of the consequences. They suffered from chronic pain, infection, and long lasting emotional distress, including depression, anxiety, and post-traumatic stress disorder.

Despite the end of apartheid in the 1990s, the full extent of Levin's abusive practices remained largely unknown for decades. It was not until 2014 that a former victim, Lance Corporal Andre Jons Bekker, came forward and filed a criminal complaint against Levin, leading to his arrest.

In 2015, Levin was charged with numerous counts of gross human rights violations, including attempted murder, assault, and sexual assault. He was ultimately found guilty and sentenced to 14 years in prison, though he passed away in 2020 while his appeal was pending.

The revelations surrounding Levin's actions sparked outrage and renewed calls for accountability and justice for the victims. Civil society organizations and human rights advocates demanded a thorough investigation into the military's role in these abuses and the implementation of measures to prevent such atrocities from occurring again.

Alwy M. Jones

Forced Contraception in Rhodesia (now Zimbabwe)

The forced contraception of African women on white run commercial farms in Rhodesia (now Zimbabwe) during the 1970s was a deeply unethical and discriminatory practice that violated fundamental human rights.

In the 1970s, Rhodesia was under the rule of a white minority government that enforced institutionalized racism and segregation policies known as apartheid. The commercial farming sector, dominated by white landowners, relied heavily on cheap labor from the local African population.

Depo-Provera, a long acting contraceptive injection, was introduced in Rhodesia in the late 1960s as a means of population control. However, its use quickly became a tool for oppression, as African women working on white run commercial farms were coerced or forced into accepting the injections without their full consent or understanding of the implications.

Testimonies from survivors paint a harrowing picture of the abuse and exploitation they endured. Many women reported being threatened with the loss of their jobs or housing if they refused the injections. Others were deceived, being told that the injections were routine medical treatments or vitamins.

The physical and emotional toll was immense. The side effects of Depo-Provera, including irregular bleeding, weight gain, and mood changes, were largely dismissed or ignored by the authorities. Some women experienced long term fertility issues, while others were left traumatized by the violation of their bodily autonomy.

The forced contraception of these African women constituted a grave violation of their human rights, including the right to bodily integrity, reproductive autonomy, and informed consent. It was a form of reproductive coercion, perpetrated by those in positions of power against a vulnerable and marginalized population.

This practice also had broader implications for reproductive rights in the region. It reinforced the notion that women's bodies were subject to control and manipulation, undermining efforts to promote gender equality and reproductive justice.

The legacy of this abusive policy continues to resonate today. Many survivors still grapple with the physical and psychological scars, while their communities confront the intergenerational impacts of limited family sizes and disrupted cultural practices.

Furthermore, the forced contraception of African women on commercial farms has contributed to a climate of mistrust and skepticism towards family planning programs in some parts of Zimbabwe. This has posed challenges for efforts to promote voluntary and informed contraceptive use and reproductive healthcare access.

Despite the historical injustices, there has been limited accountability for those responsible for the forced contraception of African women in Rhodesia. Calls for official acknowledgment, apologies, and reparations for the survivors and their families have largely gone unheeded.

Alwy M. Jones

Sterilization Experiments in German South-West Africa (now part of Namibia)

Eugen Fischer's sterilization experiments on Herero women in German South-West Africa (now Namibia) during the colonial period represent one of the darkest chapters in the history of medical ethics and human rights abuses.

In the early 20th century, German South-West Africa was a colony of the German Empire. The indigenous Herero and Nama people faced systemic oppression, discrimination, and violence at the hands of the colonial authorities. The genocide of the Herero and Nama peoples between 1904 and 1908, known as the Herero and Namaqua Genocide, was a precursor to the atrocities committed by the Nazis during the Holocaust.

Eugen Fischer was a German anthropologist and eugenicist who conducted pseudoscientific experiments on the Herero and Nama peoples in the colony. His "research" was rooted in the racist and discredited ideology of racial hygiene, which sought to promote the supposed superiority of the "Aryan race" and justify the subjugation and oppression of indigenous populations.

Fischer's sterilization experiments targeted Herero women, whom he considered to be of "mixed race" due to their perceived racial intermixing with Europeans. These women were subjected to invasive medical procedures, including the surgical removal of their reproductive organs, without their consent or proper understanding of the implications.

The physical and psychological trauma inflicted on the Herero women who underwent forced sterilization was immense. Many experienced chronic pain, infection, and long term health complications as a result of the procedures. The loss of their fertility was a devastating blow, not only to their personal well-being but also to the cultural and social fabric of their communities.

The experiments were a blatant violation of human rights, bodily autonomy, and the fundamental principle of informed consent in medical practice. The victims were treated as mere subjects for Fischer's racist and pseudoscientific agenda, with complete disregard for their dignity and well-being.

Fischer's sterilization experiments on Herero women were part of a larger pattern of colonial oppression, exploitation, and dehumanization of indigenous populations. These experiments laid the foundation for the subsequent development and implementation of the Nazis' eugenics program and their horrific atrocities against Jews, Roma, and other persecuted groups during the Holocaust.

The legacy of these experiments continues to resonate today, as communities in Namibia and elsewhere grapple with the intergenerational trauma and ongoing consequences of colonial violence and oppression.

In recent years, there have been growing calls for accountability and reparations for the victims of Eugen Fischer's sterilization experiments and the broader colonial atrocities committed against the Herero and Nama peoples. Survivors and their descendants have demanded official recognition, apologies, and compensation from the German government and for these crimes against humanity to be properly acknowledged and addressed.

Alwy M. Jones

The Racist Rhetoric that Should Have Ended a Political Career

In late summer 1971, a routine heads of state meeting took a bigoted turn with implications that would later stain Ronald Reagan's political career. Reagan, then governor of California, was paying a formal call on President Richard Nixon in the Oval Office of the White House. Their conversation was being recorded, unknown to them at the time, via one of the very same voice operated recording systems that would later upend the Nixon presidency during the Watergate scandal.

The details of what was said during this encounter did not come to light until 2019, when historians reviewed the recordings. What was revealed demonstrated an unmistakable streak of anti-Black prejudice and ignorance about race relations in the United States; a damning indictment of both leaders.

The audio captured Reagan referring dismissively to "Blacks" as he proceeded to baselessly stereotype the entirety of African UN representatives with a vague claim that they were actively engaging in a "massive conspiracy" against the United States for reasons of domestic American politics. Not only were such allegations nonsensical in regards to the largely ceremonial role of UN ambassador, but they attributed a broad degree of sophistication in plotting and execution to individuals Reagan was openly painting as underserving of sovereignty over their own nations.

Meanwhile, Nixon could be overheard on the same tape actively validating and extending Reagan's characterization of Blacks serving in African governments as "by nature" real life Idi Amins or Bokassas; a reference to the authoritarian dictators then leading Uganda and Central African Republic, respectively. He further claimed that leaders of various African nations harbored a "hatred of Whites" that rendered them complicit in anti-White uprisings in the Caribbean.

In essence, two White, Western leaders drew an unmistakable racist line separating "Blacks", even the educated, ambitious, and relatively modernized descendants of anti-colonial Africa from their own standards of human character and national competency. Blacks were presented in their minds not as people in command of their own destinies or sovereign states, but as an indistinguishable continental mass prone to hatred, intellectual inadequacy, and the cultivation of violence.

The very existence of this thinking among political elites was disturbing. But it was rendered all the more abhorrent given its shaping of actual policy, Nixon's Benghazi line referenced a fear of post-colonial disintegration that resulted in Blacks being systematically excluded from academic institutions, jobs, and other opportunities. There was severe blowback from Reagan's slur when it surfaced in 2019, with the Reagan Foundation having to apologize.

But for many, this captured a moment when two supposedly revered elder statesmen showed the stunning prejudices they held toward those of another race. More importantly, it underscored the realities that racism, covert bias, and denial of the worth and humanity of another racial group remain a critical conversation topic for today's younger generation to address fully. Only then will the scourge of hate be forever smashed.

RONALD REAGAN: Last night, I tell you, to watch that thing on television as I did...

RICHARD NIXON: Yeah.

REAGAN: ...To see those monkeys from those African countries. Damn them. They're still uncomfortable wearing shoes.

NIXON: (Laughter) Well, and then they - the tail wags the dog there, doesn't it?

REAGAN: Yeah.

NIXON: The tail wags the dog.

Alwy M. Jones

Operation Gladio

Operation Gladio, a clandestine NATO "stay-behind" operation, has become synonymous with Cold War intrigue and allegations of false flag operations. Initially conceived as a contingency plan against potential Soviet invasion, evidence suggests it evolved into a more complex and controversial program.

Established in the late 1940s, Operation Gladio involved setting up secret armed resistance networks across Western Europe. While officially intended to activate in case of Soviet occupation, investigations have revealed a darker side to its operations.

Several incidents in Western Europe during the Cold War have been linked to Gladio operatives, with allegations that these were false flag operations designed to be blamed on communist or left wing groups:

1. Piazza Fontana bombing, Italy, 1969: Initially blamed on anarchists, later investigations implicated right wing groups with possible links to Italian intelligence services.

2. Oktoberfest bombing, Germany, 1980: While officially attributed to a lone right wing extremist, some investigators have suggested broader involvement.

3. Brabant killings, Belgium, 1982-1985: A series of violent attacks initially blamed on criminals, later suspected to have connections to Gladio networks.

Motives:

1. Creating a "Strategy of Tension": Vincenzo Vinciguerra, a convicted Italian terrorist, stated: "The reason was quite simple: to instill fear in the center of society... to create a situation of such tension as to require a turn to the right and the introduction of an authoritarian state."

2. Discrediting the Left: By attributing violent acts to communist or left wing groups, these operations aimed to erode public support for such ideologies.

3. Justifying Military Buildup: Dr. Daniele Ganser, author of "NATO's Secret Armies," argues: "These operations served to justify increased military spending and to maintain a climate of fear necessary for NATO's continued relevance."

Consequences:

1. Political Landscape: These operations contributed to a rightward shift in some European countries, particularly Italy.

2. Public Perception: They fostered a climate of fear and mistrust, shaping public opinion against left wing ideologies.

3. Military Expansion: The perceived threat helped justify NATO expansion and increased defense spending.

4. Democratic Erosion: Some scholars argue these activities undermined democratic processes by manipulating public opinion through violence.

Expert Opinions:

Dr. Leopoldo Nuti, Cold War historian: "Operation Gladio represents a dark chapter in transatlantic relations, raising serious questions about the methods used to combat communism."

William Blum, former State Department employee: "The full truth about Gladio may never be known, but its existence reveals the lengths to which governments were willing to go in the name of anti-communism."

Operation Gladio and related covert activities had profound impacts on Cold War Europe, potentially shaping political landscapes through fear and manipulation. While some details remain classified or disputed, the uncovered evidence suggests a complex web of covert operations that went far beyond their stated defensive purposes.

These revelations continue to influence discussions about government accountability, the ethics of covert operations, and the long term consequences of manipulating public perception for geopolitical aims.

Levon Affair AKA Operation Susannah

Operation Susannah was a covert Israeli operation carried out in Egypt in 1954. The operation involved a group of Egyptian Jews who were recruited by Israeli military intelligence to plant bombs in various locations frequented by Western civilians in Alexandria and Cairo, including cinemas, libraries, and American diplomatic facilities.

The primary goal was to create chaos and instability in Egypt, potentially disrupting negotiations between Egypt and Britain over the withdrawal of British troops from the Suez Canal zone. By framing these attacks as the work of local Egyptian dissidents, Israel hoped to sour relations between Egypt and Western powers, particularly the United States and Britain. Israel believed that a continued British military presence in Egypt would serve as a buffer against potential Egyptian aggression.

The operation, however, was a spectacular failure. Egyptian authorities uncovered the plot, arresting and trying the operatives. Two were executed, and the others received long prison sentences.

The incident became known as the Lavon Affair, sparking years of controversy and internal political strife in Israel. The affair severely damaged trust between Israel and Egypt, reinforcing Egyptian suspicions about Israeli intentions in the region. The affair increased suspicion towards Egyptian Jews, many of whom subsequently left the country.

Alwy M. Jones

Cannibalism in Europe

Cannibalism, the act of humans consuming human flesh, has a complex history in Europe. While often associated with distant, "primitive" cultures, evidence suggests it has played a role in European societies throughout history.

Ancient and Classical Period:

Greek and Roman sources mention cannibalism among certain groups:

1. Herodotus described the Androphagi or "man-eaters" north of the Black Sea.

2. Some Roman accounts accused druids of ritual cannibalism, though these claims are disputed.

Dr. Miranda Aldhouse-Green, archaeologist: "While some accounts may be exaggerated or propaganda, ritual cannibalism can't be ruled out in certain ancient European contexts."

Medieval Europe:

Cannibalism during this period was often associated with extreme circumstances:

1. Siege of Ma'arra (1098): Crusaders reportedly resorted to cannibalism due to starvation.

2. Great Famine (1315-1317): Some chronicles mention cannibalism as a desperate measure.

Early Modern Period:

Medicinal cannibalism became prevalent:

1. Mumia: Powdered mummy was used as medicine across Europe.

2. Blood drinking: Fresh blood was believed to cure epilepsy.

Dr. Richard Sugg, author of "Mummies, Cannibals and Vampires": "Medicinal cannibalism was widespread and socially accepted in early modern Europe, practiced even by royalty."

Modern Era:

Instances of cannibalism in modern Europe are rare and usually associated with extreme situations or mental illness:

1. Siege of Leningrad (1941-1944): Some residents resorted to cannibalism during the Nazi blockade.

2. Armin Meiwes case (2001): A German man killed and ate a voluntary victim, raising complex legal and ethical questions.

Cannibalism in Europe has a long, complex history that challenges simplistic narratives. From prehistoric survival to early modern medicine, it has taken various forms. While no longer practiced openly, its cultural impact persists, influencing literature, law, and ethical debates.

The Surveillance of Pedro Albizu Campos

In the 1930s, the FBI conducted extensive surveillance on Pedro Albizu Campos, a prominent Puerto Rican independence leader, and his Nationalist Party. This operation, hidden for decades, had far reaching consequences for both Albizu Campos and the Puerto Rican independence movement.

The FBI, under J. Edgar Hoover's direction, began monitoring Albizu Campos and the Nationalist Party in the early 1930s. This surveillance was part of a broader program targeting perceived subversives and radicals.

Dr. Federico Subervi, media and political communication scholar: "The FBI's interest in Albizu Campos stemmed from his vocal opposition to U.S. control of Puerto Rico and his ability to mobilize supporters."

The Surveillance Methods Included:

1. Infiltration: FBI informants were placed within the Nationalist Party.

2. Wiretapping: Phone conversations were monitored.

3. Mail interception: Correspondence was intercepted and analyzed.

Albizu Campos was convicted twice on charges of seditious conspiracy; in 1936, sentenced to 10 years in federal prison and in 1950, arrested after an unsuccessful nationalist revolt, sentenced to 80 years.

These convictions were heavily influenced by evidence gathered through FBI surveillance, raising questions about the fairness of the trials.

In the 1980s, Congressman Luis Gutierrez brought this surveillance to public attention:

"The extent of the FBI's involvement in suppressing the Puerto Rican independence movement was shocking. It was a clear violation of civil liberties and democratic principles."

The FBI's surveillance of Pedro Albizu Campos represents a controversial chapter in U.S.-Puerto Rico relations. While ostensibly aimed at preserving national security, these actions raised serious questions about civil liberties and the right to political dissent. The legacy of this surveillance continues to shape Puerto Rican politics and identity today.

Alwy M. Jones

Civil Rights, KKK Violence, and FBI Shadows

On March 25th 1965, Viola Liuzzo, a white civil rights activist from Detroit, was murdered by Ku Klux Klan members in Alabama. The subsequent investigation and its aftermath exposed disturbing aspects of FBI operations during the civil rights era.

Viola Liuzzo, 39, was shot and killed while driving on Highway 80 in Lowndes County, Alabama, after participating in the Selma to Montgomery voting rights march. Four Klansmen were in the car that pulled alongside Liuzzo's vehicle and opened fire.

The FBI quickly identified the suspects; Collie Leroy Wilkins Jr, William Orville Eaton, Eugene Thomas and Gary Thomas Rowe Jr.

Gary Thomas Rowe Jr. was revealed to be an FBI informant who had infiltrated the Klan. This discovery raised questions about the FBI's methods and the extent of their prior knowledge of Klan activities. The revelation that Rowe was an FBI informant complicated the case significantly. It brought the FBI's tactics under scrutiny and raised questions about their priorities in monitoring civil rights activities versus Klan violence.

Following Liuzzo's murder, the FBI, under J. Edgar Hoover's direction, engaged in a campaign to discredit her;

1. Communist Allegations: The FBI spread rumors suggesting Liuzzo had Communist ties.

2. Drug Addiction Claims: False information about drug use was circulated.

3. Interracial Relationship Insinuations: The FBI promoted unfounded rumors about Liuzzo's relationship with African American activists.

Declassified documents reveal direct communication between FBI Director J. Edgar Hoover and President Lyndon B. Johnson regarding these insinuations:

1. Hoover-LBJ Calls: Records show Hoover personally called Johnson to share unsubstantiated claims about Liuzzo.

2. Autopsy Information: Hoover provided Johnson with selective autopsy details that could be misconstrued to support the drug use allegations.

The communication between Hoover and Johnson demonstrates how high up the chain these smear tactics went. It wasn't just low-level FBI operatives; this was a concerted effort from the top.

The murder of Viola Liuzzo and its aftermath expose a dark chapter in FBI history, revealing how the bureau, under J. Edgar Hoover, prioritized discrediting civil rights activists over pursuing justice. This case continues to raise important questions about law enforcement accountability, the ethics of informant use, and the intersection of government agencies with social movements.

Alwy M. Jones

WikiScanner: Unmasking the Editors behind Wikipedia's Curtain

In August 2007, Virgil Griffith, then a graduate student at the California Institute of Technology, released WikiScanner, a tool that exposed the organizations behind anonymous Wikipedia edits. This development sent shockwaves through the online community and beyond.

WikiScanner is a database that combines Wikipedia's edit logs with IP address data, allowing users to see which organizations are making anonymous edits to Wikipedia articles.

One of the most notable discoveries was that computers from FBI networks were used to edit the FBI's own Wikipedia article. These included removing critical information and adjusting language to paint the FBI in a more favorable light. This raised questions about potential conflicts of interest and the manipulation of public information by government agencies.

WikiScanner also revealed numerous instances of companies editing articles related to their products or competitors; for example employees at Diebold, a voting machine manufacturer, were found to have removed paragraphs detailing criticisms of their products.

The tool also exposed edits made from government IP addresses across various countries, often on politically sensitive topics.

WikiScanner demonstrated the vulnerability of crowd sourced information to manipulation, but also showed the power of transparency in countering such manipulation.

WikiScanner's release in 2007 marked a significant moment in the evolution of online information and transparency. By exposing the sometimes hidden agendas behind Wikipedia edits, it raised crucial questions about the integrity of crowd sourced knowledge and the responsibility of organizations in the digital age. While Wikipedia has since implemented stricter policies, the lessons from WikiScanner continue to inform discussions about trust, transparency, and accountability in online spaces.

Alwy M. Jones

The Overthrow of the Hawaiian Kingdom

On January 17th 1893, Queen Liliʻuokalani, the last monarch of the Hawaiian Kingdom, was deposed in a coup d'état that would ultimately lead to the annexation of Hawaii by the United States. The events leading to this pivotal moment were years in the making.

The coup was orchestrated by a group of businessmen and plantation owners, many of American origin, who formed the Committee of Safety. This group, led by Sanford Dole, claimed that the Queen's attempt to promulgate a new constitution threatened American lives and property in Hawaii.

American sugar planters were concerned about the McKinley Tariff of 1890, which eliminated the advantages Hawaiian sugar had previously enjoyed in the U.S. market. Annexation by the U.S. would solve this problem. The U.S. government also recognized Hawaii's strategic value in the Pacific, particularly the deep water port at Pearl Harbor. Some Americans viewed the acquisition of Hawaii as a natural extension of U.S. expansion across the continent.

The role of the United States in the overthrow is a matter of historical controversy. U.S. Minister John L. Stevens, with the backing of American warships in Honolulu harbor, recognized the new Provisional Government almost immediately. Marines from the USS Boston were landed ostensibly to protect

American lives and property, but their presence effectively supported the coup.

Queen Liliʻuokalani, hoping to avoid bloodshed, yielded her authority under protest, stating her belief that the United States would eventually restore Hawaii's sovereignty. This hope would prove unfounded.

The impact of these events on Hawaii has been profound and long-lasting. The overthrow ended the Hawaiian monarchy and eventually led to Hawaii becoming the 50th U.S. state in 1959. However, it also sparked a Hawaiian sovereignty movement that continues to this day.

Annexation solidified American economic dominance in Hawaii, particularly in the sugar and pineapple industries. It also paved the way for Hawaii's eventual transformation into a tourist destination. The overthrow accelerated the decline of Native Hawaiian culture and language. However, recent decades have seen a resurgence of interest in preserving and revitalizing Hawaiian cultural practices.

The controversial nature of these events was officially recognized in 1993 when the U.S. Congress passed the Apology Resolution, acknowledging the overthrow as illegal and offering a formal apology to Native Hawaiians.

Alwy M. Jones

Annexation of Texas and California by the United States from Mexico

The story begins with Texas, which declared its independence from Mexico in 1836 after a revolt by American settlers. For nearly a decade, Texas existed as an independent republic, but its fate was far from settled.

The belief that the U.S. was destined to expand across the continent fueled support for annexation. The Southern states saw Texas as potential new slave territory, while the Northern businesses eyed its cotton production. The fear of British influence in an independent Texas pushed the U.S. to act.

President James K. Polk, elected in on a pro-annexation platform, moved swiftly to bring Texas into the Union. This action, along with a dispute over Texas's southern border, led directly to war with Mexico in 1846.

The Mexican-American War (1846-1848) was the crucible in which the fate of California was forged. U.S. motivations for acquiring California included; California's coastline offered valuable harbors for trade with Asia.

Though the Gold Rush hadn't yet begun, California's potential was recognized. Acquiring California would stretch the U.S. from "sea to shining sea."

As American forces advanced into Mexican territory, a group of American settlers in California staged the

Bear Flag Revolt in 1846, declaring an independent California Republic. This short-lived entity was quickly absorbed by advancing U.S. forces.

The war concluded with the Treaty of Guadalupe Hidalgo in 1848. Mexico ceded nearly half its territory to the United States, including California, New Mexico, and parts of several other future states. The U.S. paid $15 million in compensation and agreed to assume $3.25 million in Mexican debt.

The U.S. grew by more than 500,000 square miles, fulfilling its "Manifest Destiny." The newly acquired territories intensified the debate over slavery's expansion, contributing to pre-Civil War tensions. Tens of thousands of Mexicans suddenly found themselves living in U.S. territory, facing discrimination and loss of land rights despite treaty guarantees.

The discovery of gold in California in 1848 sparked a massive influx of settlers and rapid economic development.

The influx of American settlers led to further displacement and conflicts with indigenous peoples. The war strained U.S.-Mexico relations for decades and influenced Mexico's future development.

Alwy M. Jones

The "Manifest Destiny"

Manifest Destiny was essentially a justification for genocide. It positioned indigenous peoples as obstacles to be removed in the name of 'progress' and 'civilization. The consequences were devastating; forced relocations, broken treaties, and the systematic destruction of Native cultures and ways of life.

Manifest Destiny, a term coined by journalist John L. O'Sullivan in 1845, encapsulated the idea that American expansion across the continent was both inevitable and divinely ordained. This belief provided a moral veneer to actions that today we recognize as profoundly unjust.

The impact on indigenous communities was catastrophic, Manifest Destiny led to policies of forced assimilation, such as the Indian Boarding School system, which aimed to 'kill the Indian, save the man.' These schools tore children from their families, forbade them from speaking their native languages, and attempted to erase their cultural identities. The intergenerational trauma from these policies is still felt in Native communities today.

But the legacy of Manifest Destiny extends beyond its direct impact on indigenous peoples. The idea of American exceptionalism, the belief that the U.S. has a unique mission to spread democracy and freedom, can be traced back to Manifest Destiny. This mindset has shaped U.S. foreign policy for generations, often with problematic results.

Manifest Destiny promoted the idea of nature as something to be conquered and exploited. This attitude has contributed to environmental degradation and climate change, issues we're grappling with today.

Confronting the legacy of Manifest Destiny is crucial for addressing ongoing injustices. Understanding this history is essential for making progress on issues like land rights, tribal sovereignty, and cultural preservation. It's not just about the past, it's about shaping a more just future.

There is a growing recognition of the need to teach a more complete, nuanced history of westward expansion in schools. This includes acknowledging the perspectives and experiences of indigenous peoples, which have long been marginalized in traditional narratives.

Alwy M. Jones

Indian Boarding School System

The Indian Boarding School system, operational from the late 19th to the mid-20th century, was designed to forcibly assimilate Native American children into Euro-American culture. The schools' ethos, infamously articulated as "Kill the Indian, Save the Man" by Richard Henry Pratt, sought to eradicate indigenous languages, cultures, and identities.

The boarding school experience created a rupture in Native communities. Children were torn from their families, forbidden to speak their languages or practice their cultures. This severing of cultural ties and family bonds has led to cycles of trauma that they're still grappling with today.

Many indigenous languages are now endangered or extinct due to the schools' English only policies. Generations of Native Americans grew up disconnected from their traditional practices and beliefs. The lack of parental role models in the schools led to difficulties in family relationships and parenting. High rates of depression, anxiety, and substance abuse in Native communities are often linked to this historical trauma. Many Native communities still harbor deep mistrust towards formal education systems. They told them their ways were evil, that they had to become 'civilized'.

The federal government has also begun to acknowledge its role. In 2021, Secretary of the Interior Deb Haaland, the first Native American to serve as a cabinet secretary, launched an initiative to investigate the history of these schools and their ongoing impacts.

Despite these efforts, challenges remain. Many communities still struggle with the long term effects of the boarding school system, from high poverty rates to ongoing battles over land rights and sovereignty.

YouTube

WhatsApp

Buy Me Coffee

Alwy M. Jones

Milton Keynes UK
Ingram Content Group UK Ltd.
UKHW020832231024
450026UK00014B/361